Ketogenic Diet for Be

The Ultimate Guide to Lose Weight and Gain a Healthy Lifestyle. Reset your Metabolism and Burn Fat Enjoying the 30 Days Meal Plan.

Victoria Green

Table of Contents

Introduction

The ketogenic diet is based on the idea that the body will burn fat to heat, optimizing weight reduction by depleting carbohydrates, the main energy source. The body transforms carbohydrates into glucose or blood sugar, which it uses to produce electricity after eating foods that contain carbohydrates. Glucose is often used for energy before the body is converted into fat processed for food since its simple energy form.

The aim of the ketogenic diet is to limit carbohydrates consumption to break down fat for strength. As this happens, the liver breaks down fat to create ketones that are by-products of the metabolism. In the absence of glucose, these ketones are used to heat the muscle. However, when you start the Keto Diet, the essential. Consistency is the thing to consider. You can find it challenging, of course, to enjoy cheat food anytime there is a decent chance, such as on vacation and an outing with friends. While you will rebound back on time, you must keep your body as close as possible when switching to diets that the higher metabolism will sustain your body.

That's the choice! You enter many individuals that, like yourself, have selected an active diet and can enjoy all the advantages which the Keto diet will have to offer. It contains

well-established recipes & tips on making Keto recipes fast and simple. It gives you all you need to learn from equipment, ingredients and storage recipes. It provides nhe traditional Keto recipes band365 recipes that make the Keto diet the cake!

Why the Ketogenic Diet option?

Investigators have, over the years, learned that the alternative of the keto diet has many advantages. There was early concern that the diet would induce a build-up of cholesterol in the body, thereby contributing to cardiovascular disease due to the high saturated fat of the foods eaten by those on a diet. Nevertheless, as more and more scientists have studied the diet, they have discovered intrinsic benefits of starting this diet. For one, instead of carbs for nutrition, the body can use fat. Therefore, since there is such a limited volume entering the bloodstream, the body would not depend on carbohydrates and will instead retain the ketones-the fats-for subsequent energy usage. The idea that the stomach may not be as hungry is another plus, and those on the Keto Diet are also at a reduced risk of going behind their regimen by snacking. Since the Keto Diet promotes the intake of many foods high in protein that serve to curb hunger. The person runs into a ketosis mode,

which is normal for those who consistently fast, and does not need a lot of food to keep things running. What's better than having a good diet and not having frequent pangs of hunger? Finally, the wellness improvements that the Keto Diet provides are remarkable. Following the Keto Diet, people avoid entirely starchy carbs, including bread and pasta, and replace non-starchy vegetables such as asparagus, carrots, broccoli, and many others. Vitamins & nutrients that sustain a balanced body, and are also far lower in calories, are filled with these types of foods. The Keto Diet is also prescribed for cancer patients and treating people suffering from conditions such as epilepsy. A study has demonstrated, in regions in the body in which there is a lot of glucose; it's what carbohydrates are, cancer cells flourish. Therefore, if the body consumes fewer carbohydrates, there'll be less glucose, and cancer cells would not expand and thrive afterward.

It will place the body in a "ketosis," condition, where the organ has become a fat burner rather than consuming sugar. Fortunately, a keto diet, for starters, or keto fundamentals, is simple to follow. This is how it works for the keto diet:

1. Diminish one's carb intake.

2. Improve the consumption of healthy fats that contribute to the development of satiety.

3. It is now meant to burn fat and produce ketones without glucose accumulating in the bloodstream.

4. Ketosis is legally done when ketone levels in the blood rise to a certain degree.

5. This condition leads to slow, relatively rapid weight loss before the body reaches a secure and stable weight.

What is a Keto-like diet?

A very low-carb diet method developed by studies working with epilepsy patients at the Johns Hopkins Medical Centre in the 1920s is the classic ketogenic diet. Fasting, in addition to providing certain positive effects on body weight, blood pressure, cholesterol, and hunger levels helped to minimize the number of seizures suffered by patients by restricting the consumption of all foods over a short duration (such as prolonged fasting), particularly those that contain carbohydrates. Unfortunately, long-term fasting is not a practicable option if used for more than a couple of days, for this reason was developed the keto diet, to mimic the same beneficial fasting benefits.

The keto diet for beginner's works by "tricking" the body to act as if it were fasting by removing only the glucose found in

carbohydrate foods (while reaping intermittent fasting benefits). The standard keto diet under several different names is now referred to as "low-carbohydrate" or "quite ketogenic diet" (LCKD or VLCKD for short).

<u>**On a Keto Diet, What You Can and Can't Eat**</u>.

These are some of the items you should consume on a ketogenic diet after the high-fat, low-carb rule:

- Oils and fats (olive oil, butter, coconut oil, etc.)

- Avocado

- Full-fat dairy (cream cheese, cheese, sour cream, etc.)

- Low-carb vegetables above ground level (mushroom, asparagus, broccoli, etc.)

- Seeds and nuts

- Meat (preferably organic and grass-fed)

- Seafood (tuna, salmon, scallops, crab, etc.)

- Eggs

These are some of the foods that if you are consuming keto, you can keep away from:

- Fruits

- The Sweets (ice cream, candy, cake, honey, cookies, etc.)

- Cereals (rice bread, pasta, oats, etc.)

Vegetables (potatoes, beets, carrots, etc.)

Keto Diet Vs Regular Diet

Why choose the keto diet to other diets out there? A significant part of the decision is the state of health and preference regarding whether you can hold on to the recommended regimen. The ketogenic diet surmonted a standard American diet without exercise, almost like a standard American diet with no workout.

Reasons for the Keto Diet to Try

The main reason for being on Keto is that you are unhappy with your weight. The ketogenic diet is specifically directed at weight loss/weight gain/weight protection, rather than any other health effects, because of its focus on eating fat. The ketogenic diet is mainly used as a short-term weight loss solution rather than a long-term lifestyle.

Another common reason people try the keto diet may be that they have epilepsy. Curiously enough, the ketogenic diet has also been used to manage seizures, especially for children who do not respond to traditional drug therapy.

Other nutritional advantages associated with the Keto diet

Apart from the potential to lose weight, there are various other theoretical effects to the keto diet. There have been studies about how, to name a few, the keto diet can treat coronary heart disease, neurological disease, autism, type 2 diabetes, polycystic ovarian syndrome and acne. Do you suffer from one of these medical conditions and wish to see if the keto diet can help? You should verify the diet is safe.

Beginning your diet for Keto.

The first step in starting the keto diet to see if the diet is healthy is to consult a doctor. When the doctor gives you the go-ahead, you can figure out how much sugar, fat, and protein, you should eat every day. This trio is referred to as the "macronutrients," or macros, and is a word you will often encounter if you intend to go Keto.

To verify how much of each macro you can drink, you can use a keto calculator that calculates your age, ethnicity, height, and weight. The calculator would tell you how many ounces of carbohydrates, proteins and fats to consume per day and how many calories to eat per day in general. With these macro numbers in mind, please cook your meals correctly.

Chapter 1: Introduction to The Ketogenic Diet

A very low sugar, high-fat diet, which has certain similarities with the Atkins & low carb diets, is the ketogenic diet. It requires significantly lowering and replacing the intake of carbohydrates with fat. This carbohydrate reduction places the body in a metabolic condition called ketosis. Our body becomes incredibly good at burning fat for energy as this happens. It also converts fat into ketones in the liver, which can give the brain with energy. Large diminutions in blood sugar and insulin levels can result from ketogenic diets. This has some health effects, along with elevated ketones.

A ketogenic diet carries the body into a "ketosis" mode, a physiological state that happens when much of the energy in the body occurs from ketone bodies in the blood, rather than glucose from foods produced from carbohydrates (like grains, all sources of sugar or fruit, for example). This contrasts with a glycolytic condition, where much of the body's fuel is produced by blood glucose (sugar) (or energy). This condition can also be reached by several days of absolute fasting, but beyond a couple of days, that is not permanent. (That's why some beginners' keto diet programs incorporate extended fasting

with keto to better impact weight loss.) While dietary fat (incredibly saturated fat) also gets a bad reputation, creating fear of weight gain and heart disease, when carbohydrates are not readily available, it is also your body's second preferred source of energy.

How Do You Get Into Ketosis?

Too many people are wondering, is this keto diet working? Yeah, of course, but only if you can get ketosis from your body. In a keto diet for beginners, here and you'll get your body into ketosis, then start burning body fat for starters:

1. Glucose intake from carbohydrate foods (grains, vegetables, fruit, etc.) is reduced.

2. This causes the body to find an alternate fuel supply: fat (think avocados, coconut oil, and salmon).

3. Meanwhile, the body often begins to burn fat in the absence of glucose and thus produces ketones.

4. You enter a ketosis point until ketone levels in the blood increase to a certain amount.

5. This state of high ketone levels results in rapid and steady weight loss before a safe, stable body weight is achieved.

Beginning to wonder how many carb foods you can drink and "in ketosis" still be? For people with epilepsy, the conventional

ketogenic diet was around 75 percent of calories from fat products (such as oils or fatty meat cuts), 5 percent from carbs and 20 percent from protein. A less strict version for most people (what I call a "modified keto diet") will also help encourage weight loss in a healthy, and sometimes very fast, way.

Usually, aiming for around 30-50 net grams is the suggested amount of total carbs to start with to transition and stay in this state. This is considered a more mild or versatile approach, but, to begin with, it can be less daunting.

You can opt to reduce carbs even further if you like (maybe only from time to time), down to around 20 grams of net carbs every day, until you're more used to "eating keto." This is considered the standard, "strict" quantity to be adhered to by many keto dieters for best performance, but note that each is slightly different.

1.1. History Of The Keto Diet

The keto diet is a lower-carb, modest protein; higher fat diet focused on findings and a tradition dating back to the early 1900s. For weight loss, many people prefer the keto diet. However, Keto was first detected in epilepsy prevention, and many other effects remain, such as improved neurology,

enhanced emotional clarity and constant stamina during the day. What is the history of this popular lifestyle, and why is its appeal increasing dramatically? We look at the history, progression and importance of the keto diet.

Early Beginnings: Fasting

Your body will continue to generate ketones from stored fat if you quick (don't eat anything for some time) to make up for the loss of sugar/carbohydrate energy. As early as around 500 BC (1), our ancestors understood the health advantages of fasting, unintentionally inducing a state of ketosis and leveraging it for a range of conditions. There are only a few known historical accounts of fasting as medical care below.

- Ancient Greek physicians used fasting to cure ailments.

- As the only epilepsy cure, Hippocrates reported fasting.

- Benjamin Franklin wrote, "Resting and fasting are the best of all medications."

- Mark Twain wrote, "A little hunger can do more for the average sick person than the best drugs and the best doctors can do." I do not mean a limited diet; I mean one or two days' absolute abstention from food.

- Fasting was used to treat type 1 and type 2 diabetes in 1914.

- An osteopath named Hugh Conklin fasted for up to 25 days for several children with epilepsy in 1922, supplying only minimal fluids.

The Birth of Keto: A Less Rigid Treatment for Epilepsy

A doctor named Russell Wilder of The Wilder Clinic recognized the risks of fasting for kids in the early 1920s and investigated various diets to see whether anything else could elicit a reaction comparable to fasting. He found that by preventing fructose and eating a higher fat diet, you would replicate fasting symptoms. He tried this diet on patients with epilepsy (with an excellent result), and, for several years, his diet became the primary cure for epilepsy. The birth of the ketogenic diet was Wilder's invention.

New anti-convulsion seizure medications were discovered in the 1930s. Patients and clinicians found it easier to take medicine than to make lifestyle changes, so these experimental medications became the primary therapy for epilepsy.

The Keto Diet's Second Coming

It was not until the 1970s that the ketogenic diet was revived when customers showed interest in weight loss and dieting. Yet her comeback was not instantaneous. The following timeline shows the gradual but steady rise in popularity and use of Keto.

1972: The book Dr. Atkins' Diet Revolution, written by a cardiologist called Dr. Atkins, describes his years of academic findings into low-carb diets for weight loss and cardiac wellbeing. This positions on the map the higher fat/low-carb type of feeding.

1977: Dr. Phinney, a psychiatrist and scientist who spent his life findings nutrition, wrote The Last Chance Diet, a book that advocated a diet he created for fat and protein beverages. However, this drink he made lacked the requisite minerals and individuals became ill, some even dying.

1988: Dr. Phinney introduces The Optifast Diet, a dietary regimen based on products he developed for fat and protein drinks, but this time with minerals in it. Oprah backs it, and keto science has picked up.

1990: U.S. news network NBC broadcasts a documentary about a two-year-old child recovering from extreme epilepsy on the beneficial outcome of the ketogenic diet. The show is instigating a vast increase in keto-related PubMed publications.

1992: An update to the 1972 book by Dr. Atkins is published. It encourages other physicians to write dieting books focused on similar low-carb concepts, dubbed Dr. Atkins New Diet Movement, which marks the beginning of the 'low-carb craze.'

1996: A movie starring actress Meryl Streep and sparking a revived scientific curiosity in the ketogenic diet is the kid's story from NBC's 1990 TV special.

2000s (early): The Atkins Diet is rediscovered, and the low-carb campaign gains support.

2013: The anti-aging and health effects of a ketogenic diet were seen in a Science magazine report. In the Paleo and biohacking cultures, this induces an intense curiosity about Keto.

2015: Popular podcaster Tim Ferris interviews on "Fasting, Ketosis, and the End of Cancer" with Dr. D'Agostino, Ph.D., a keto findings scientist ketogenic diet to the top of Google diet searches, where it has been ever since.

The Keto Diet Today

During the last five years, there has been an explosion in the keto diet for personal use and clinical investigation. The trend of the five-year Google search term has gradually grown and continues to grow.

How does Keto stick around? Since there are mounting health benefits. The three main reasons why people choose Keto:

Weight loss:

One big reason many individuals turn to Keto is the benefit of weight loss. In the absence of carbs, fat is burned as fuel by your

liver. During the day, fat as fuel keeps you healthy and happy, and you want fewer calories. It also burns extra fat and lets you lose weight quickly if you consume under the standard prescribed macros (calories broken down into fractions of fat, protein, and carbs).

Brain Health:

The brain is fond of ketones. A keto diet aids other neurological disorders, such as Alzheimer's and Parkinson's, instead of epilepsy. Concentration, attention, concentration, comprehension, and reduced brain fog are all improved by Keto.

Cancer:

As adjunctive therapy for cancer, experts are findings, Keto. Results are positive up to now. Keto substantially improved lifetime and reduced tumor development in recent findings. (8) Pancreatic, colon, brain, prostate, gastric, neuroblastoma and lung cancers were tumor forms.

1.2. Truth About Carbs And Fat Loss

The subject of much debate was the low carbohydrate diet. It is so common to cut carbohydrates, though, is that it is an easy way to drop the pounds.

Besides food for vital organs, such as the liver, central nervous system, and brain, carbohydrates are the primary energy source for the body. For the body to function optimally, healthy carbs, such as so-called complex carbohydrates, are essential.

They break down carbohydrates into a primary source of energy called glucose. To bring glucose into the cells, the body uses insulin. The blood sugar level increases as too many sugars are eaten, insulin rises, and weight gain is often the product.

What is a low-carb diet?

Low-carb diets can lead to fast weight loss, but side effects may arise.

By restricting their carbohydrate food options, low-carb diets restrict the number of calories a person gets. This contains carbohydrates that are both good and evil. To compensate, low-carb diets tend to be richer in proteins and fats.

Carbohydrates are the primary source of nutrition for the body. The body burns its reserves of protein and fat for food as this supply is decreased.

Low-carb diets have been shown to contribute to accelerated weight loss, such as the Atkins diet and the Dukan diet. These diets, though, are strict and may have specific harmful side effects.

When lowering carbohydrate consumption to help reduce weight, it might be healthier to take a more moderate method for most persons.

What amount of carbs and calories should people eat to lose weight?

Although several findings show that low carb diets facilitate accelerated weight loss, this weight reduction is always short-term.

Recent findings reinforce the belief that a high-quality diet doesn't just require managing calories from carbohydrates. Instead, dieters should pay attention to how much calories, including carbohydrates, protein, and fats, are consumed from all food products to achieve a healthier balance.

Dieters have been shown to compare the multiple weight losses arising from a low-fat diet (LFD) to a low-carb diet in a new survey (LCD). The findings observed that weight improvements were comparable for both the LFD and LCD categories after six months of adopting calorie-reduction diets.

The Americans' Dietary Guidelines prescribe that the total daily calories of an adult come from the following:

- 45–65 percent carbohydrates

- 10–30 percent protein

- 20–35 percent fat

Some nutritionists suggest a combination of 40 percent carbs, 30 percent protein and 30 percent fat as a successful goal for safe weight loss. A calorie diet of 1,500 with 40 percent carbohydrates converts from sugars to 600 calories a day. An individual on this diet will have to consume 150 g of carbohydrates per day using a proportion of 4 calories per gram (g) of carbs. It will also contain 450 calories or 112 g of protein and 450 calories or 50 g of fat a day in this 1,500 calorie diet. People should also be mindful that everybody has somewhat different requirements when it comes to nutrients like carbs.

The primary interests of individuals will differ depending on their height, weight, and levels of exercise. A diet may works for one person but cannot inherently work for another person. Before beginning, individuals must address any weight loss diet or calorie limits with a practitioner.

Good carbs vs. bad carbs

Carbohydrates, as they maintain at the right weight, are critical for health. It's important to remember that, though, not all carbs are the same.

Carbohydrates are widely referred to as either "good carbs" or "bad carbs." Carbohydrate consumption can concentrate on

good carbs over bad carbs when following a balanced diet, especially when trying to lose weight.

Good carbohydrates

Fiber vegetables are an example of healthy carbohydrates, such as sweet potatoes. Complex carbohydrates are healthy carbs, meaning that they are rich in fiber and minerals that take longer to break down. They should not trigger blood sugar levels to surge or climb too high since they take longer to break down.

Examples of good carbs include:

- high-fiber beans and legumes
- high-fiber vegetables, such as sweet potatoes
- whole fruit with the skin on
- whole grains

Bad carbs

Bad carbohydrates are essential carbs that have been readily broken down and cause `blood sugar levels to rise rapidly.

Examples of bad carbs include:

- white sugar, bread, pasta, and flour

- sugary drinks and juices

- cakes, candy, and cookies

- other processed foods

Takeaway

It's safe to consume carbs in their standard, high-fiber type. Weight gain can result from packaged foods that are high in white sugar and refined carbohydrates.

Ideal weight management can be achieved by measuring calories from sugars by observing a proper combination of complex carbohydrates, proteins, and healthy fats. The fastest way to lose weight is by combining dieting, exercise, and improving behavior or lifestyle at the Academy of Nutrition and Dietetics. Registered dieticians will provide recommendations to someone who wishes to make improvements to help them lose weight. Anyone concerned about reducing their carb consumption and consuming more protein and fat should track their saturated fat intake. Too much of this, as well as the chance of heart failure, will raise cholesterol levels.

13 low-carb fruits and vegetables

Fresh fruits and vegetables are low-fat and low-calories food, but they contain differing quantities of sugar and carbohydrates. Carb material is valuable to learn for individuals seeking to control their intake. Data suggests that

consuming a variety of fresh fruits and vegetables, including cancer, heart disease, and type 2 diabetes, will help minimize the risk of the most common causes of sickness and death.

A specific carb intake is expected by many diets and eating plans. For starters, people adopting the ketogenic diet tend to eat about 20-50 grams (g) of 2,000 calories per day of carbohydrates. Eating the following fruits and vegetables without canceling out a low carb diet's health benefits will add color, taste, and essential nutrients.

Fruits

Since they contain naturally occurring carbohydrates, Fruits appear to have a higher carbohydrate content than other crops. This does not mean, though, that individuals should stop them. People tracking their consumption of carbohydrates should also remember that certain fruits have a higher amount of water. This suggests that per 100 g serving, they have fewer carbohydrates.

Some low carb fruit solutions are the following.

1. Watermelon

This summer fruit has the least carbohydrate size, with just 7.55 mg/100 g of fruit.

It is also a rich vitamin A source and has high water content, making it good for high volumes.

Although offering fewer calories, watermelon can also contribute to feelings of fullness.

2. Strawberries

For individuals observing their carb consumption, berries are a common alternative, and strawberries have the least of any berry. 7.68 g of carbohydrates are given per 100 g serving of strawberries. They are also excellent potassium and vitamin C sources.

3. Cantaloupe

A typical summer fruit, this orange melon contains just 8.16 g of carbohydrates per 100 g. Some people love eating melons with tuna salad, including cantaloupe and honeydew. To make a cooling water Fresca, try mixing it with lime, mint, and water.

4. Avocados

Fruits with relatively low carbohydrate content are avocados. An individual gets an average of 8.53 g of carbohydrates for every 100 g of avocado. Avocados are a decent source of mono-unsaturated fats, too. These may have cardiac and blood vessel safety effects.

5. Honeydew

For a 100 g, another form of melon, honeydew, offers about 9.09 g of carbohydrates. As well as potassium, it is also an excellent source of vitamin C. Potassium is an electrolyte that helps maintain adequate blood pressure, regulate acid levels, and support a balanced metabolism.

6. Peaches

Peaches are among the sweeter fruits available, have a relatively low carbohydrate content. An individual gets 9.54 g of carbohydrates for every 100 g of fruit. Serve the peaches with some cottage cheese for a low carb snack, or try a peach and blueberry smoothie.

Vegetables

For every diet, vegetables are an essential source of nutrients. As part of a carb-controlled diet, they are handy for supplying nutrients while limiting carbohydrates' intake. They are rich in fiber and smaller than any other food category in total calories per meal. They also include a large variety of beneficial compounds, including phytochemicals, vitamins and minerals. The higher the water level, the lower the carb content is per 100 g serving, in general. For the fewest calories, the following are the vegetable options.

7. Cucumbers

Cucumber in every salad is a refreshing and nutritious addition. A cucumber contains only 2.16 g of carbohydrates per 100 g serving when a person peels the skin. Cucumbers with attached skin have 3.63 g of carbohydrates, rendering them a low carb vegetable of the highest rank, whether or not they want to consume the skin.

However, the most nutrients of a cucumber are contained in the flesh. People should attempt to eat the skin along with the remainder of the cucumber for this purpose. Those pursuing a carb-controlled diet should prefer a thin-skinned form of a cucumber, such as a Persian cucumber. English cucumbers, which will increase the carb count, tend to have thicker skin.

8. Iceberg lettuce

Iceberg lettuce is inferior in overall nutritional value, is perhaps one of the most common vegetables. The iceberg lettuce, though, has just 2.97 g per 100 g of carbohydrates.

9. Celery

Celery is a nutritious vegetable that goes well in casseroles and salads. The same amount of carbohydrates are given by this vegetable as iceberg lettuce (2.97 g per 100 g). As part of every low-carb diet, it will bring a pleasing crunch to several meals.

10. White mushrooms

Mushrooms give just 3.26 g of carbohydrates per 100 g. For a balanced, low carb meal, humans should add them to an egg-white omelet. Any literature shows that mushrooms can maintain heart health and decrease the risk of specific type 2 diabetes and cancers.

11. Spinach

3.63 g of carbohydrates are given for every 100 g of spinach. That amounts to only about 1 g per cup. An important source of iron, calcium, and magnesium is Spinach, it can be particularly useful in a vegetarian or vegan diet to complement these essential minerals. People can use spinach to boost salads, pasta dishes, and wraps.

12. Swiss chard

Swiss chard is another nutrient-dense leafy vegetable. It offers just 3.74 g of carbohydrates for each serving of 100 g. In soups or sautéed with garlic, people will enjoy Swiss chard.

13. Tomatoes

Tomatoes are a legume type. For every 100 g, they only contain 3.89 g of carbohydrates. Tomatoes are incredibly flexible. They can be eaten raw, fried, or put into a salad by humans. They are not only tasty, but they can also reduce the risk of stroke in a person.

Myth 1: Your Body Goes Into Ketoacidosis

Reality: Ketosis is what causes the Keto to burn fat.

You get into ketosis while you go on a keto diet, a physiological condition where the body uses fat for food (rather than glucose, its preferred energy source). The body smash down fat and turns it into ketone bodies during this process. This is not equal to diabetic ketoacidosis, a diabetes condition that develops because, according to the Mayo Clinic, the body does not get enough insulin and ketone levels are elevated at the same time.

Myth 2: You Can Continue And Stop And Still Keep The Weight Off

Reality: Keto seesawing would only bring you back to losing all the weight.

Audrey Fleck, RDN, an integrative and holistic dietician nutritionist and licensed

Myth 3: Everyone Has The Same Carb Needs

Diabetes instructor in Perkasie, Pennsylvania, says that Keto has become such a fad that people don't realize what they're getting into and rush into the diet. Because of this, one day, individuals sometimes observe the keto diet and then consume carbohydrates the next, she says. But this way, you're not going to reap the possible rewards of prolonged ketosis.

Reality: How many carbohydrates you can eat depends on your health.

You may not know how low it is in carbohydrates before you initiate a very-low-carb diet like Keto. Followers usually eat 20 to 50 grams (g) of carbohydrates a day, frequently starting to help the body reach ketosis at the lower end of the range. Nonetheless, you might be able to go higher based on conditions (like physical activity), says Fleck. She suggests teaming up with a nutritionist who can measure your food requirements. What's more, it's not essential to go to Keto often, she says. "Some people have genetic problems with the use of fat for energy, making it even harder or ineffective for them to diet," Fleck says.

Myth 4: With Keto You Can Eat As Much Bacon And Butter As You Want

Reality: In your diet, Keto calls for prioritizing unsaturated fat. Yes, a diet high in fats is Keto. But that doesn't mean that in the morning, you're going to cook up a pound of bacon. "In White Plains, New York, dietician Jill Keene, RDN, says, "The ketogenic diet doesn't give you the green light to consume all sorts of fats. Limiting saturated fats, such as bacon and sausage, and loading the diet with heart-healthy unsaturated fats, such as avocados, olive oil and flaxseed, along with almonds in moderation, is the healthiest way to stock up on fats.

Myth 5: Veggies And Fruits are High In Carbs, You Can't Eat Them On Keto

Reality: To prevent constipation, a nasty keto side effect, you need to eat the produce.

Carbohydrate forms contain fruits and vegetables. (Oils, butter, and beef are the only products that would be carb-free.) But that doesn't mean you can skip producing. These raw, unprocessed foods are essential sources of vitamins, antioxidants, and fiber, the latter of which, a frequent keto side effect, is crucial for preventing constipation. Keene recommends No starchy vegetables such as zucchini, cauliflower, cucumbers, tomatoes, and broccoli, plus small quantities of lower-carb fruits such as berries, think of strawberries, raspberries, and blueberries. That said, certain healthier foods that are not included in the keto diet are still available, so you'll want first to check the general list of keto diet foods.

Myth 6: A Keto Diet Is A Plan That Is High In Protein Reality

It's low-carb, but the Atkins Diet is far from here. Throwing a bowl of eggs and smoked salmon together for breakfast and a large cut of steak for dinner sounds like it's on time, but you need to eat protein in moderation. "Abundance protein can be transformed into glucose, taking your body out of ketosis, spiking your blood sugar," Keene says. (This is the difference between Keto and Atkins.) What's more, she points out, "protein breakdown of amino acids can also lead to higher ketones, which can be problematic for a keto dieter who already has high ketone levels in her body," she says. A licensed dietician will help lead you to the correct macronutrient breakdown if you are uncertain of how much you can eat.

Myth 7: The Best Way To Lose Weight: Keto Diet

Reality: For everyone, there's no correct diet.

Only because your buddy effectively lost weight on Keto (or it seems as if everyone is talking about it) doesn't mean that Keto is the right diet for you. "The biggest misnomer I have come across in my practice is that the end-all, be-all answer to weight loss is [a keto diet]," says Keene. There are many fashionable

diets out there, but, she says, success comes from having an eating plan to which you can adhere. "I help my clients find a way to eat that they feel good about, don't obsess about, and get them to their goals," says Keene. (In fact, findings published in November 2015 in the journal Cell indicated that people have varying blood sugar reactions to the same things, but no one diet is the solution.). We know we're harping a lot on talking to a licensed dietician about all this, so you should do exactly that before going to Keto.

1.4. Different Types Of Keto Diet

There are many iterations of the keto diet. Three popular ones are:

- The Standard Ketogenic Diet (SKD)

- The Cyclical Ketogenic Diet (CKD)

- The Targeted Ketogenic Diet (TKD)

The variations in each diet are discussed below and the purposes of making changes, and for whom the diet may be beneficial.

The Standard Ketogenic Diet (SKD)

As mentioned above, a high-fat, low-carb, and moderate-protein diet is the traditional keto diet. It is one of a handful of diets (Paleo, Atkins) that sparked a rise in popularity in low-carb diets due to its undeniable results, especially weight loss.

Below are a few general recommendations that, aside from the cyclical and targeted keto diets, set the standard ketogenic diet:

- Until you are finished and do not have to count calories, you eat

- Usually, you eat the same thing every day (actual food items will vary, but the macronutrient split outlined earlier will be the same or similar)

- You usually eat three meals a day, but this can vary, although (there is no set time for meals)

Drawbacks

You use the body to work off glucose, so there is usually a transition time after transitioning to a keto diet. Fatigue, dehydration, and other "keto flu" effects are encountered by many people, which tend to go away after a week or two.

The Cyclical Ketogenic Diet (CKD)

The cyclical ketogenic diet is a regular keto diet where one or

you deliberately deviate by eating clean carbs (between 100 and 150 grams). two days per week This provides a carb "cycle" that can then be used in exercises to increase performance. While many athletes (like our partner Tim Tebow) use the traditional ketogenic diet, the CKD is aimed at athletes or someone who exercises regularly.

Although keto-friendly supplements such as exogenous ketones can be used instead of glucose to improve performance, your performance can benefit from consuming more carbs, particularly during long-term workouts. Some findings also indicate that eating carbohydrates, particularly after workouts, will increase the ability to add fresh muscle (although a tailored ketogenic diet could also aid.

Drawbacks

The most significant consideration (and possible drawback) of CKD is that you will not be in ketosis on days where you eat extra carbohydrates. Clean carbs or not, before it switches on to ketones for food, the body has to be drained of muscle glycogen. It's equally important to remember that it may take longer than just one day to get back into ketosis if you don't exercise sufficiently. You will not immediately re-enter ketosis simply because you slip down to 50 grams of carbs the next day. From two to three days are needed before you get back into

ketosis, depending on how healthy you are. So while this strategy will boost efficiency, it won't technically be a ketogenic diet if you aren't careful.

The Targeted Ketogenic Diet (TKD)

A regular keto diet where you take nutrient timing into account is the intended ketogenic diet. You still eat 5-10% of your daily calorie intake of carbohydrates to help you stay in ketosis, unlike the CKD. But you deliberately eat some carbs before and after exercise to help fuel your efficiency instead of the traditional ketogenic diet. It has been shown that eating carbohydrates before exercise increases efficiency. And eating carbs in combination after a workout (within 45 minutes) will accelerate regeneration and increase the session's health gains.

Drawbacks

Again, if you eat all 50 grams of carbs before a workout, you could have a killer training session. But right after your workout, you do not get into ketosis again either.

It would help if you were careful to keep in ketosis, like the CKD (a ketone home monitoring kit can help). Another thing to remember about TKD is that those foods would be off-limits for much of the day. You definitely can't consume fruit and veggies or even higher-carb nuts the rest of the day if you eat

any of the 50 grams of carbohydrates before and after workouts. This could make adherence to the keto diet challenging, depending on the degree of discipline. A TKD could strengthen teaching, but it might not be worth it if it's too hard for you to do regularly.

2.1. Keto Best Foods

KETO FOOD LIST

VEGETABLES

- Arugula
- Spinach
- Leafy greens
- Eggplant
- Mushrooms
- Broccoli
- Lettuce
- Cauliflower
- Zucchini
- Asparagus
- Artichokes
- Bell peppers
- Fennel
- Radishes
- Sauerkrut
- Onions
- Cabbage
- Celery
- Brussels sprouts
- Green beans
- Kale
- Garlic
- Kimchi
- Boy Choy
- Jalapeno peppers

SEAFOOD

- Bass
- Octopus
- Shrimp
- Snails
- Cod
- Clams
- Halibut
- Flounder
- Eel
- Haddock
- Scallops
- Anchovies
- Red Snapper
- Lobster
- Mussels
- Sardines
- Salmon
- Squid
- Sole
- Trout
- Tuna
- Mackerel
- Catfish

DAIRY

- Parmesan
- Mozarella
- Cottage cheese
- Glee
- Milk
- Eggs
- Sour cream
- Full fat cheese
- Greek yogurt
- Cream
- Butter
- Brie cheese
- Feta cheese
- Goats cheese
- Ricotta

FRUITS

- Tomatoes
- Avocado
- Blackberries
- Raspberries
- Blueberries
- Strawberries
- Coconut
- Lemon
- Limes
- Olives

MEATS

- Beef
- Bison
- Bacon
- Chicken
- Turkey
- Quail
- Pheasant
- Ham
- Veal
- Boar
- Buffalo
- Deer
- Duck
- Venison
- Elk
- Lamb
- Rabbit
- Moose
- Pork

NUTS & SEEDS

- Almonds
- Pine nuts
- Pecans
- Pumpkin seeds
- Walnuts
- Hazelnuts
- Brazil nuts
- Macadamia nuts
- Hemp seeds
- Chia seeds
- Sesame seeds
- Sunflower seeds
- Flaxseeds

These are the 21 staple keto foods that you need to continue your health journey, so read through and take notes. Although the items that you should consume are almost limitless as part of your keto diet, this 21-item grocery list covers the basics to get you started.

KETO SHOPPING LIST

Meats:
Bacon
Ground Beef
Beef
Chicken (all cuts)
Turkey
Pork
Wild Game
Duck
Beef Jerky
Sausages
Ham
Pastrami
Pepperoni
Smoked Deli Meats
Hotdogs
Fish & Shellfish

Eggs:
Eggs

Dairy:
Butter (grass fed preferred)
Heavy Cream
Hard Cheeses
Soft Cheeses
Sour Cream
Cottage Cheese
Greek Yogurt (low carb)
Mayo

Flour:
Coconut
Almond
Psyllium Husk

Veggies:
Artichokes
Asparagus
Broccoli
Brussels Sprouts
Cabbage
Cauliflower
Celery
Cucumber
Garlic
Green Beans
Kale
Lettuce
Mushrooms
Okra
Onion
Peppers
Pumpkin
Radishes
Sauerkraut
Spinach
Tomatoes
Zucchini

Fats:
Avocado Oil
Coconut Oil
Olive Oil
MCT Oil
Ghee
Lard
Bacon Fat
Cocoa Butter

Fruits:
Avocados
Berries
Lemon
Lime
Coconut (unsweetened)

Nuts & Seeds:
Pecans
Almonds
Walnuts
Macadamias
Peanuts (your choice)
Sunflower Seeds
Chia Seeds
Flaxseeds
Pumpkin Seeds

Unsweetened Nut Butters:
Almond Butter
Macadamia Nut Butter
Coconut Butter
Peanut Butter (your choice)

Pantry Items:
Pork Rinds
Chicken Broth
Beef Broth
Bone Broth
Xanthan Gum
Herbs & Spices
Tabasco
Salad Dressings (low carb)
Braggs Aminos
or Coconut Aminos
Baking Cocoa Powder
Sweetener Options -
Swerve (granulated
or confectioners),
Stevia,Erythritol,
Monk Fruit, Truvia, Xylitol
100% Unsweetened
Chocolate
Lily's Choc Chips
Pickles
Parchment Paper

kasey trenum

www.kaseytrenum.com
facebook: easyketolowcarbrecipes

The end aim of a keto diet is to induce dietary ketosis, a physiological condition where, instead of carbs and sugar, your body burns processed fat for power. With a list of foods to stop on Keto, we are here to help you achieve your goal.

FOODS TO AVOID ON A KETO DIET

GRAINS

Wheat
Rice
Barley
Oats
Quinoa
Millet
Buckwheat
Rye
Bulgur

BEANS/ LEGUMES

Green Peas
Lima Beans
White Beans
Cannellini Beans
Pinto Beans
Fava Beans

MOST FRUITS

Apples
Bananas
Pineapple
Kiwi
Cherries
Watermelon
Mangoes
Grapes
Pears
Papayas
Oranges
Tangerines

STARCHY VEGETABLES

Potato
Carrots
Peas
Sweet Potato
Parsnip
Corn
Yucca
Yams

SUGARS

Honey
Maple Syrup
Agave Nectar
Corn Syrup
Cane Sugar
Raw Suga

FATS/ OILS

Margarine
Vegetable Oil
Canola Oil
Soybean Oil
Corn Oil
Grapeseed Oil
Peanut Oil
Sesame Oil
Sunflower Oil

OTHER

Milk
Processed Foods
Low Fat -
Dairy Product

You will make the necessary changes to continue living your low-carb lifestyle so that you know which things to eliminate on keto. For lower carb advice, you can also check out our keto compliant food list.

For decades, low-carb diets have become contentious. Some people believe that these diets increase cholesterol and cause heart disease because of their high-fat content. In most scientific findings, however, low-carb diets show their benefit as safe and helpful.

Here are 16 proven advantages of ketogenic diets for wellness.

1. The Origins of the Ketogenic Diet: Treating Epilepsy

Epilepsy is a (neurological) central nervous system condition in which brain function becomes erratic, causing irregular actions, sensations, and often lack of memory during seizures or cycles. Epilepsy is a nervous system condition in which one experiences sporadic, capricious convulsions. That is a result of irregular motion in the human brain. Physical side effects such as muscle fits, spasms and emotional signs such as erratic behavior, irregular thoughts, etc., may be integrated into epileptic seizures.

In some children who do not respond to epileptic drugs, the ketogenic diet is an extraordinarily viable cure for Epilepsy. To prevent seizures, a few children may produce better results using the ketogenic diet than other children. The ketogenic diet is authentic and genuine. It fits very well for many people. The catch is that it's intensely demanding and hard to execute. It is so hard to follow that most physicians prescribe it only for patients who could not manage their prescription seizures. The keto diet is high in fats, so it allows kids to drink four times the amount of protein or carbohydrate fat calories. It is a strict diet to follow, to be frank. Not every one of the nutrients a body requires is given by this diet, so your young person will most likely need to take sugar-free vitamin supplements.

How Does Ketogenic Diet Work For Epilepsy?

There is an age-old association between ketogenic dieting and Epilepsy. A century-old tradition has been to treat Epilepsy with a ketogenic diet. In reality, to treat Epilepsy, the keto diet was initially and predominantly used. It needs a great deal of time and vigorous therapy to Treat Epilepsy with medications. It has become a century-old practice to cure Epilepsy with a ketogenic diet, and in reality, the keto diet started as an epilepsy remedy. The body must use fat for nutrition, a process

called ketosis, by decreasing the number of carbohydrates that a person consumes.

A viable method for minimizing the number of seizures in children with Epilepsy is the ketogenic diet. Be sure to frequently track its efficacy while you are adopting a ketogenic diet to treat Epilepsy. Epilepsy can be treated with the Ketogenic diet, and its effects can be managed and even reversed.

2. Boosts Brain Functions:

In the 1920s, the ketogenic diet was introduced as a treatment method to alleviate seizures in pediatric epilepsy situations. Although we did not completely understand the mechanisms of how this occurred, it was recognized that elevated blood ketone levels were associated with a substantial reduction in epileptic events. Since then, we have understood more profound ways of enhancing brain function through a ketogenic diet. In recent years, after people discovered that they would have more stamina and elevated mental acuity when adopting it, the ketogenic diet re-merged. Humans are learning the facts after years of sideways findings stating that the body must have a steady supply of carbohydrates to be healthy.

In addition to better mental results, the ketogenic diet as a treatment tool for mental illness and neurodegenerative disorders is also emphasized. The following are some of the disorders:

Mitochondrial Biogenesis When it comes to it, to carry out its tasks, the body requires electricity. This energy comes in ATP, provided mainly by mitochondrial structures that occupy almost every cell in your body. Cells have much more mitochondria in some parts of the body than the rest, representing the required amount of energy to function correctly.

The brain is amongst these regions. You provide a substantially more significant energy amount by improving the mitochondria's number and energetic production in your brain. This, in itself, will offer many of the advantages of brain stimulation. Many of the most promising approaches for controlling mitochondrial biogenesis include fasting and a ketogenic diet.

1. Less Oxidative Stress

Oxidative stress is helpful in limited doses, but the mitochondria can be very dangerous in abundance. Inflammation and reduced mitochondrial energy production are created by prolonged oxidative stress. Since oxidative stress induces damage at the mitochondrial level, any cell in your body can be negatively affected.

Also, since the brain is so focused on healthy mitochondria, the effects of excess oxidative stress are the first to suffer. Oxidative stress in the mitochondria is a normal by-product of the development of electricity. In contrast to glucose metabolism, ketone metabolism has been shown to produce much lower oxidative stress levels, essentially reducing inflammation and encouraging mitochondrial health. This eventually results in an increased output of electricity. Neurodegenerative diseases characterized by demyelination, such as multiple sclerosis, are believed to be positively affected by systemic inflammation, for yet another cause, rendering the ketogenic diet a suitable treatment.

2. Glutamate GABA Balance

Glutamate and GABA are two very significant neurotransmitters that are responsible, respectively, for concentration and relaxation. A healthy interplay between these two needs proper neurological function.

Brain conditions such as autism, Lou Gehrig's, Amyotrophic Lateral Sclerosis (ALS), Epilepsy, and mood disorders have been linked with a deficiency of these neurotransmitters, sometimes manifesting with an abundance of glutamate. In comparison, those with excess glutamate and low GABA levels will appear to feel nervous, have difficulties sleeping, and

experience brain fog. If it continually overstimulates brain cells, chronically elevated glutamate is exceptionally inflammatory. Excess glutamate can be transformed into GABA in a stable individual to better balance neuronal functions. It has been shown that maintaining a ketogenic diet helps to promote this conversion. Improved concentration and reduced levels of stress and anxiety are the direct consequences of this.

3. Increases energy

The fat and ketone bodies of virtually all the body cells can be used to supply food. There will be a noticeable boost in energy as you escape the ups and downs associated with high-carbohydrate/high-glucose/high-insulin levels that result in feeling sluggish and exhausted during the day until the body use ketones as its primary fuel supply. In the absence of glucose, which is typically used as a fast energy supply for cells, the body tends to burn fat and instead creates ketone bodies (this is why the keto diet is also referred to as the ketone diet). You enter a state of ketosis after ketone levels in the blood increase to a certain amount, which typically leads to fast and steady weight loss before you achieve healthy, stable body weight.

These high in fat acids are then smashed down by the body into an energy-rich material called ketones, circulating through the

bloodstream. Via the mechanism called ketogenesis, fatty acid molecules are broken down, and a particular ketone body called acetoacetate is formed and energy supplied. The result of the "ketone diet" is to stay fuelled by circulating high ketones (which are also often referred to as ketone bodies), and is responsible for modifying your metabolism in a manner that some people want to say turns you into a "fat-burning machine." Being in ketosis is somewhat different in terms of how it feels physically and emotionally and its effect on the body.

4. Decreases inflammation and pain

Inflammation plays a significant role in the body's ability to repair itself and remain protected from disease and another injury. Yet so much inflammation, like chronic conditions that become crippling for certain persons, may have severe repercussions.

The way it can be anti-inflammatory is one of the positive facets of the ketogenic diet. Many people look to ketosis to better control and minimize inflammation symptoms. This topic is all about how ketosis and the best anti-inflammatory ketogenic diets should decrease inflammation.

How Ketosis Reduces Inflammation

Being in ketosis guarantees that the body uses fat for energy instead of sugar, and you've already learned that sugar is inflammatory. Sugar in excess leads the body to:

- Producing high concentrations of insulin
- Raising markers of inflammation
- Create free radicals, compounds that can inflame the blood vessels' linings, and activate the body's immune response.
- Triggering chronic condition

Eating a very low sugar ketogenic diet tends to halt insulin spikes from unregulated sugar levels that increase blood sugar and create inflammation throughout the body. Let's take a closer look at the relationship between infection, cancer, and suffering, mostly from both, to understand this better.

What to Avoid: Inflammatory Foods

Avoid foods that are high-sugar or have refined ingredients. Specifically, some of the essential items to avoid are here:

- Processed, frozen and refined foods. Soy products, condiments, and prepared meals are included. (It's best to stick as far as possible with foods that don't need a label.)

- High-glycaemic foods such as refined sugars, cereals (yes, including whole grains), fruit, and starchy vegetables

- Refined vegetable oils such as maize, safflower, and soybean oils, especially those high in inflammatory omega-6s,

- Coffee and tobacco, as both may both be inflammatory. Continue to adhere to herbal tea or water.

While inflammation is part of our biological processes, when it is triggered chronically in the body repeatedly, leading to illness and debilitating symptoms, it becomes an issue. Ketosis and the ketogenic diet will function in our bodies as an outstanding normal, food-based means of fostering an anti-inflammatory condition.

5. Increases Performance

It is not unusual for those adopting a ketogenic diet to note a reduction in their results upon the introduction of the diet. Although all of these decrements seem to vanish as keto-adapted. However, there are also some scenarios where efficiency can become compromised, and it is necessary to have

successful strategies to resolve these circumstances! Some years ago, I experimented the ketogenic diet on Cross Fit athletes. I have learned some techniques from those experiences, as well as following a ketogenic lifestyle myself that can improve success on a ketogenic diet:

1. Stay Hydrated

Insulin levels appear to be lower because of lowered glucose consumption by following a ketogenic diet. Low insulin levels allow the kidneys to excrete further sodium and urine, contributing to an elevated risk of dehydration for ketogenic athletes if they may not drink sufficient quantities of water during the day.

- Fix: Improving efficiency on a ketogenic diet includes drinking a glass of water when you wake up.

- Its profound health effects, add a splash of fresh lemon juice and a splash of apple cider vinegar for the additional vitamin c and antioxidants.

Consume at least 1/2 of your body weight in ounces a day as a guideline. For starters, you can drink at least 75 ounces (150/2 = 75) of water a day if you weigh 150 lbs. (more if you work out and sweat heavily!). This would have been about 4.5, 16.9 fl oz.

Bottles of water every day.

2. Replenish Electrolytes

Lower insulin levels will, as previously described, lead to increased excretion of water and electrolytes. It is incredibly vital to substitute these electrolytes to avoid headaches, brain fog, weakness, and muscle cramps and optimize physical and mental efficiency.

Fix: Add sea salt to your water

As it is deprived of all of the useful nutrients, avoid table salt.

Tips:

- Hold in your gym bag a Himalayan sea salt grinder at all times!

- Using a keto-friendly substitute for electrolytes

- Using enhancers of keto-friendly water containing electrolytes

- Try a pre-workout snack that is ketogenic:

- This may seem like a crazy combination, but it's one of my favorite pre-workout snacks that offers a decent dose of the electrolytes needed: potassium, sodium, and magnesium. Don't give it a knock before you try it!

- 1/2 avocado (potassium)

- 1 tbsp. Butter with almonds (magnesium)

- Himalayan sea salt dash (sodium)

3. Consume Enough Fat & Adequate Protein

Fat is FUEL! It is essential to eat enough good fats to keep your body energized and your brain concentrated during the day and throughout your workouts. Besides, sufficient protein intake is required to enhance the repair and regeneration of muscles and promote immune function.

4. Trust the Process

It takes time to become keto-adapted or "fat-adapted." It could take weeks for others and months for others. There is no clear-cut point that determines whether someone is fat-adapted entirely. However, any of the common symptoms include sustained and improved energy, increased mental focus and attention, decreased appetite, enhanced performance, and much more.

5. Exogenous (Supplemental) Ketones

The amount of ketone supplements that have entered the market in the past year has seen a massive surge. As we know, with many people referring to them as a "super fuel," ketones are a perfect source of fuel for the body and brain. The findings behind exogenous ketones are still evolving, but the great potential is shown by the impact on efficiency, therapeutics, and cognitive applications.

"The Carb Rinse"

The introduction of "carb rinse" is another possible technique for improving efficiency on a ketogenic diet. This includes taking a sip of a carbohydrate-containing liquid, such as a Gatorade sports drink, swinging it in your mouth for 5-10 seconds and finally spitting it out. Using this approach, multiple findings have shown increased results during low to high-intensity exercise. Carb rinse" is believed to activate receptors in the mouth that link to brain reward areas, leading to a decrease in perceived exertion and subsequent increase in performance effort and motivation."

Here are a few ideas to proceed if you are planning on playing with a TKD:

- Verify that you are entirely keto-adapted (this can take weeks to months, depending on the person).

- Try using the technique of "carb rinse" first.

- Start by adding 15 to 20 grams of pre-workout carbohydrates to determine resistance and energy levels. There are a couple of references here:

- Consume half a banana 30 minutes or so before your exercise (maybe add a slight amount of almond butter).

- 10-15 minutes pre-workout, eat a fast-absorbing carb source, such as gummy bears or a rice cake.

- Throughout the initial experimental process, keep track of your results, mood, hunger levels, and ketone output (optional).

6. Builds More Lean Muscles

The ketogenic diet, or Keto, has become more and more popular. It is a very low carb, the high-fat diet used by many individuals to lose weight and has various other health benefits. For a long time, many people assumed that it was impossible to build muscle on a keto diet or low carb diets in general. This is because carbs, which are known to promote insulin release, an anabolic hormone that helps shuttle nutrients into cells, are restricted by low carb diets, helping to create conditions that drive muscle growth.

How to build muscle on a keto diet

The following recommendations can help you to build muscle.

Determine your calorie intake

You need to consistently eat more calories than you burn to build muscle optimally. The amount of calories you need to eat

each day, building muscle depends on several variables, such as weight, height, lifestyle, sex, and activity levels. The first thing you need to do is determine your calories for maintenance: in order to maintain the same weight you must fix the number of calories you need to consume each day to. To do so, weigh yourself up to three times a week and use a calorie tracking app to record your food intake over the week. That's roughly your maintenance calories if your weight stays the same. It's recommended to increase your calorie intake by 15 percent above your maintenance calories when you're trying to build muscle. So, you should eat 2,300 calories per day to build muscle if your maintenance calories are 2,000 per day. It is a good purpose to adjust your calorie intake around once a month as you build muscle to account for your weight changes.

Eat plenty of protein

For muscle building, eating adequate protein is essential. That's because protein is the building block of muscles, which means that you need to consume more protein when trying to build muscles than your body breaks down through natural processes. Most findings indicate that eating 0.7-0.9 grams of protein per pound (1.6-2.0 grams per kg) of body weight is ideal for muscle building. Among keto dieters, there is some concern about consuming too much protein because it could encourage

your body to use gluconeogenesis, a process in which amino acids are transformed from protein into sugar, preventing the body from making ketones. However, findings have shown that individuals can safely consume approximately 1 gram of protein per pound of body weight (2.1 grams per kg) and remain in ketosis.

Track your carb intake

Traditionally, on a muscle-building diet, carbs make up the bulk of the calories. If you are trying to remain in ketosis, though, then you need to limit carbs. Most people need to eat less than 50 grams of carbohydrates per day to reach and remain in ketosis, although the exact value can vary. You may find that it can be useful to time your carb intake around your workouts, especially if you think your performance is impacted. This approach is known as a targeted keto diet, in which to help exercise performance, you eat your daily permitted carbs around your workouts.

7. Lose fat

If you suffer different metabolic abnormalities, including type 2 diabetes, high blood pressure, high waist-to-hip ratio, and low HDL (good) cholesterol, is a risk factor for metabolic syndrome. Many diets, including the ketogenic diet, have emerged to combat this, in which a person consumes a minimal amount of

carbohydrates. The ketogenic diet is characterized by high fat, moderate protein, and low carbohydrate. Ketosis is a metabolic state that the body enters when carbs are reduced, and fat is increased. The body begins to turn fats into ketones, which are molecules that can provide the brain with energy. The body and brain become very effective at burning fat and ketones for fuel instead of carbs after a few days or weeks on such a diet. Insulin levels are also reduced by the ketogenic diet, improving insulin sensitivity and blood sugar management.

On a ketogenic diet, staple foods include:

- Heavy cream

- Oils

- Nuts

- Avocados

- Seeds

- Low carb vegetables

- Meat

- Fish

- Butter

- Eggs

- Cheese

By contrast, it eliminates almost all carb sources, including:

- Grains

- Beans

- Potatoes

- Sweets

- Milk

- Cereals

- Fruits

- Some higher carb vegetables

- Rice

How do ketogenic diets promote weight loss?

Here is how ketogenic diets promote weight loss:

- Greater protein intake. Some ketogenic diets increase the intake of protein, which has many advantages for weight loss.

- Gluconeogenesis. Fat and protein are converted into carbs for fuel by your body. Each day, this process can burn many additional calories.

- Suppressing appetite. Ketogenic diets allow you to feel fulfilled. Positive changes in starvation hormones, including leptin and ghrelin, support this.

- Improved insulin sensitivity. Insulin sensitivity can be drastically improved by ketogenic diets, which can help improve fuel use and metabolism.

- Decreased storage of fat. Lipogenesis, the process of converting sugar into fat may be reduced thanks to Ketogenic diets, some findings suggest. This is because they store excess carbohydrates as fat. Fat is used for energy when there is a minimal intake of carbohydrates.

- Improved fat burning. Several findings have found that the amount of fat you burn during rest, daily activity, and exercise may be slightly increased by ketogenic diets, although more findings are required.

The ketogenic diet helps you at losign weight in an effective way. However, note that it's essential to ensure that you meet your calorie needs when following the ketogenic diet.

8. Reversing Type 2 Diabetes And Controlling Type 1 Diabetes

A ketogenic diet can be a way to help you lose weight by regulating your blood sugar. All of these are important for type 2 diabetes treatment and prevention. Diabetes is one of the country's most prevalent metabolic disorders. And they're on the rise. In 2015, 30.3 million Americans (9.4% of the population) had diabetes, and every year diabetes is diagnosed to 1.5 million Americans. And it's not counting the pre-diabetes millions or those that go undiagnosed. Fortunately, there is an overwhelming amount of evidence that suggests that a low-carbohydrate, high-fat, ketogenic diet can help stabilize blood sugar and get the symptoms of diabetes back on track. The keto diet will reverse type 2 diabetes, some experts say. A ketogenic diet can help reduce blood glucose levels, which can be beneficial if you have type 2 diabetes. It becomes more difficult to use the ketogenic diet for other diabetes types, such as type 1 or gestational diabetes. More below on that. With type 2 diabetes, the body is not able to respond correctly to insulin, often referred to as insulin resistance. Your cells are not able to use your blood glucose for energy because your insulin resistant. Then, in the bloodstream, the fat accumulates, aka constant, elevated blood sugar.

Because a ketogenic diet changes your system from using carbohydrates to producing and using fat ketones as food, your blood sugar will gradually start to decrease as you get through ketosis. This explains why persons who chose to adopt a

consistent ketogenic diet are starting to see significant improvements in their blood sugar and insulin levels. Similar to people without diabetes, life expectancy will also be similar. A ketogenic diet aims to improve the quality of life of Type 1 diabetes patients. Although low blood sugar is still a problem for type 1s, it tends to be much more manageable (compared to the low arising from an unnecessary insulin bolus) for those who use a ketogenic diet because the effects are not as overwhelming and mental acuity is not impaired.

How to Manage Type 1 Diabetes Following the Ketogenic Diet?

While not fresh, it is becoming more common to use a ketogenic diet to treat type 1 diabetes. Importantly, when deciding to transition from a high to a lower carbohydrate diet to better choose the right foods to control insulin dosing, you can consult with a competent healthcare practitioner.

For controlling his and his patients' blood glucose, Dr. Richard Bernstein uses 30 grams of carbohydrates per day so a very low carb ketogenic diet. When he reduced his insulin doses using a starch regimen, he learned that his blood sugar would remain in the usual range as follows:

- For breakfast, 6 grams

- 12 grams for lunch

- 12 grams for supper

The keto diet, to recap, will help:

- Improving immunity to insulin

- Decrease the fat in the blood

- Support you shed undesirable weight

- Provides more energy for you

- Inflammation lowers

9. Improves Blood Pressure

It is essential to select the best foods to control your blood pressure, mainly on medication. And it can help with a low-carbohydrate or keto diet.

Here are only a few ways to encourage high blood pressure from a low-carb diet:

1. Keto supports heart wellbeing

Cutting back on your carbohydrates can not only help you shed pounds if you have any weight to lose, but it may also promote heart health.

2. Blood Sugar is maintained by Keto

You immediately cut back on foods that induce an increase in blood sugar and insulin while eating a keto diet.

3. It's Low In Sugar

Although salt may undoubtedly play a part, there is strong reason to think that blood pressure can probably have a more significant sugar effect than salt.

As discovered earlier, insulin, which eventually contributes to hypertension, will induce sodium retention and activate the sympathetic nervous system. You prevent the potential dangers of high insulin levels in your body by following a low in sugar diet. Keto, which can increase blood pressure, is also low in fructose.

The Takeaway: Is a Keto Diet Good For Your Blood Pressure? A smart way to better control your blood pressure is to adopt a balanced keto diet. Not only can Keto keep diabetes in balance, but it also lets you eliminate some foods, such as high fructose corn syrup and other processed carbohydrates, which may increase your risk of hypertension. One region of caution: Certain foods that are keto-friendly often come into the processed food category. Making sure the diet of processed

beef, cheese and other low-quality canned foods containing high salt levels is being tracked.

10. Boosts Digestive Health

Interestingly, some evidence shows that digestive health may benefit from the keto diet.

Reduces inflammation

An immune reaction that defends the body from disease and infection is acute inflammation. However, chronic inflammation, including digestive problems such as Crohn's disease and ulcerative colitis, may lead to inflammatory disorders. Some reports indicate that the keto diet may help reduce the body's inflammation. A six-month report of 59 individuals showed that specific inflammation indicators reduced to a greater degree after a low-carb diet than after a low-fat diet. A few animal experiments give related findings.

May benefit some digestive disorders

Certain intestinal conditions can also help with the keto diet. For example, a very low-carb diet strengthened many irritable bowel syndromes (IBS), a condition that causes complications such as gas, stomach cramps, and diarrhea, in a report of 13 participants. Other findings note that it can also help to relieve

IBS symptoms by limiting particular forms of carbs known as FODMAPs.

Keto-friendly foods for gut health

As part of a balanced keto diet, you can comfortably enjoy some gut-friendly foods. Foods low in carbohydrates but rich in benefits for gut-boosting include:

- Avocadoes. Not only are avocados high in heart-healthy fats, but also in nutrition, offering a whopping 10 grams of fiber per cup (150 grams).

- Leafy greens. Vegetables such as arugula, spinach, kale, and cabbage, though rich in fiber and other useful nutrients such as antioxidants and vitamins C and K, are poor in carbohydrates.

- Oil from cocoons. Some animal findings indicate that coconut oil can decrease inflammation and strengthen the microbiome of the gut.

- Kimchi. This staple Korean dish is made from fermented vegetables such as cabbage, which improves its content of beneficial bacteria to improve gut health.

- Butter. Butter contains butyric acid, a short-chain fatty acid (SCFA) that can enhance digestive health and reduce inflammation of the intestines and inflammatory bowel disease symptoms.

11. Improves Cholesterol Level

Cholesterol has been a bad rap for decades, but cholesterol plays many important roles in the body. Cholesterol, for instance, has functions that include:

- Support in the synthesis of sex hormones (including progesterone, estrogen and testosterone)

- Developing brain structures

- Cognitive/mental function assistance, including children and older people,

- Facilitating fat-soluble food absorption (including vitamins A, E, D and K)

- Nutrients, triglycerides and other chemicals are passed to cells for energy consumption.

In the form of fatty acids (lipids) that pass through the bloodstream, cholesterol in our body is present. What's important to note about cholesterol is that it's vital to balance LDL and HDL cholesterol. To better remove LDL from the bloodstream, you also want to get higher HDL if you have higher LDL.

There are two distinct categories of LDL cholesterol, the form sometimes referred to as low cholesterol: big LDL (or pattern A) particles and small LDL particles (or pattern B).

How cholesterol levels can be affected by the keto diet?

Findings have demonstrated that a ketogenic diet can have a positive effect on cholesterol, cardiac and metabolic health levels in the following ways:

- Increases the size of LDL particles (increases pattern A), resulting in less oxidative stress.

- Improves the ratio of LDL to HDL. In other words, HDL cholesterol improves, helping to counter the effects of LDL.

- Reduces triglycerides, which are protective provided that elevated blood concentrations suggest an increased risk of stroke and cardiac problems.

- Enhances the ratio of triglycerides to HDL

- Reduces insulin resistance and helps to regulate levels of blood sugar (glucose), especially compared to high-carb diets

- Assists in reducing systemic inflammation

- Help reduce obesity by decreasing appetite and reducing calorie consumption ad libitum.

Consuming lots of healthy fats on the keto diet can raise HDL cholesterol (often referred to as the 'right type') and increase the ratio of LDL/HDL cholesterol, which are two primary general health markers. Findings suggest that Keto usually decreases triglyceride, LDL cholesterol, and blood glucose levels and decreases body mass index.

12. Reverses Heart Diseases

Your brain most likely goes straight to heart disease when you know someone with high cholesterol. Cholesterol and heart disease have been so closely connected together that one sounds like a synonym for the other sometimes. It lowers your cholesterol by replacing saturated fat from meat and butter with unsaturated fat from vegetable oil. As compared to the simple existence of LDL cholesterol in the blood, both the size of the LDL particle and the number of particles appear to play a more important role in the development of heart disease. In other terms, positive LDL and bad LDL are there. There is a greater association with heart disease for smaller, denser LDL particles than with large, fluffy LDL particles. This is because the tiny particles of LDL can reach through your artery walls more quickly and add to the plaques that inevitably lead to heart disease.

3 Reasons The Keto Diet is Heart-Healthy
Four of the main heart attack risk factors are:

- Resistance to insulin (and, if insulin resistance goes unchecked, type II diabetes)

- Inflammation

- Obesity

Ok now we examine these risk factors for heart failure and see if each of them is influenced by the keto diet.

1: Insulin resistance and type II diabetes reversed by a ketogenic diet

The association between insulin resistance and type II diabetes and heart disease risk is high. In fact, one of the seven main risk factors for developing heart disease is considered by the AHA to be diabetes. Here's the link: you have so much glucose (sugar) roaming through your bloodstream when you have insulin resistance (or diabetes). The excess glucose, combined with the nerves that regulate your blood vessels, will weaken your blood vessels over time. This will potentially relate to heart failure. People with diabetes who are 65 or older have a 68 percent risk of dying from heart disease.

2: A ketogenic diet that can minimize inflammation

More and more evidence shows that in heart disease, inflammation plays a significant role. Ketones may have anti-inflammatory properties themselves. Beta-hydroxybutyrate, one of the critical fuel sources that you use for ketosis, triggers a drastic reduction in the inflammatory response.

3: A ketogenic diet is perfect for reducing weight and battling obesity

One of the main causes to heart disease is obesity. Obesity, a frequent cause of heart disease, is also related to a large left heart ventricle. A ketogenic diet is an excellent choice if you're trying to shed any weight. Not only can you lose excess pounds, but the appetite will also drop, meaning that you won't wander around eating candy. A review involving more than 19,000 obese patients showed that the easiest way to induce rapid weight loss was by using a keto diet.

That is very rare, and it points to how sustainable a ketogenic diet is. Most people recover weight. The findings revealed no side effects and found that the keto diet was a healthy, efficient and affordable cure for obesity.

13. Treatment For Polycystic Ovary

The most common endocrine condition affecting women is

Polycystic Ovary Syndrome (PCOS). We discuss some interesting findings to treat this paper's condition and the association between the ketogenic diet and PCOS.

Most importantly, the ketogenic diet is known for its effect on weight loss, Epilepsy, type 2 diabetes, neurological conditions and even certain cancer types. However, for many additional conditions, such as PCOS, Keto is now being considered due to emerging findings and anecdotal evidence. Besides the fact that it would dramatically enhance health criteria to remove excess glucose from the diet, low-carbohydrate diets are exceptionally effective in lowering insulin concentrations and insulin sensitivity. Since the ketogenic diet can boost insulin sensitivity and support weight loss, findings have begun to report the diet to treat PCOS in women. It is promising, although the findings are limited; a 2005 report in a small group of obese women diagnosed with PCOS found that limiting the intake of carbohydrates to 20 grams or less per day over 24 weeks resulted in:

- Reduction in body mass of 12 percent

- 22% drop in testosterone

- Reduction in LH/FSH ratio of 36 percent

- 54% drop in fasting levels of insulin

While these results show proof of concept for the use of the ketogenic diet for PCOS, possibly the most remarkable finding was that amid prior fertility problems, two women from the report were pregnant during the report! Several clinicians have implemented the ketogenic diet as a cure for PCOS since these findings were written, several anecdotal accounts have been documented, and many trials are in development to provide further insight.

14. Reverse Non-Alcoholic Fatty Liver Disease

Exactly as it looks like is fatty liver disease: you accumulate so much liver fat. It's natural to store some fat for your liver. When you're low on gasoline, you can use stored liver fat to generate steam. When fat creeps up to more than 5 percent of the liver's weight, the issue emerges. This is considered a fatty liver disorder.

Two major forms of fatty liver disease exist:

- Alcoholic liver fat syndrome, caused by too much alcohol, and

- Lifestyle and diet-related non-alcoholic fatty liver disease (NAFLD)

It will lead to a more extreme non-alcoholic steatohepatitis disorder if you do not deal with NAFLD (NASH). As an alarm sign, you should think of NAFLD. You have extra fat in your liver, but there is no scarring and minimal or no inflammation present. Usually, easy NAFLD won't hurt your liver. But you might end up with NASH if you don't fix NAFLD and it keeps getting worse. This is where it gets ugly. Your liver gets inflamed with NASH and begins to scar, and your liver cells start to die off. Cirrhosis or liver cancer may contribute to this inflammation and injury. NASH is produced by about 7-30 percent of people with NAFLD. You consume relatively little carbohydrates on a low-carbohydrate ketogenic diet and get the rest of the calories from fat and protein. If you heard earlier, insulin and carbohydrates play a crucial role in fatty liver progression. A low-fat, high-carbohydrate diet will worsen your fatty liver, particularly if you eat tons of sugar. So, when you're adopting a ketogenic diet, what with all the dietary fat you eat? Can a diet rich in fat lead to a fatty liver?

The conclusion is no, according to a few recent reports.

De novo lipogenesis produces much of the fat that accumulates in the liver (DNL). DNL happens when the body creates fat from extra carbs or protein. There is no lack of evidence that shows the liver and metabolic health effects of a low-carb diet. There are a lot of highlights here:

- One findings showed that six months on a ketogenic diet

  resulted in substantial weight loss and progress in obese patients with fatty liver disease. Patients lose an average of 28 pounds at the end of six months and had their liver inflammation and injury significantly reversed.

- Safe patients adopting a low-carbohydrate diet had a substantial drop of liver fat in only 10 days in another findings.

- Two weeks on a ketogenic diet in a third trial induced a 42 percent drop in liver fat in NAFLD persons.

- More trials are also supporting the possible advantages of adopting a ketogenic diet and metabolic syndrome markers, including NAFLD.

- Finally, a randomized controlled report of 45 NAFLD patients showed that it has a positive effect on liver enzymes and serum fibrinogen, a protein that is usually high in more extreme cases of NAFLD, after a low-carbohydrate diet.

You don't have sugar or fructose to transform into liver fat in the carbohydrate limitation in a keto diet. You also guard against insulin resistance, which further defends against the fatty liver.

15. Helps Cancer Patients

With many trying to lose weight while consuming foods like bacon and eggs, the fashionable and often divisive keto diet has become popular. The diet, which is rich in protein and low in carbohydrates, was created to support people with Epilepsy in the 1920s. Today, experts are trying to see whether there may be other medicinal uses for the diet over a century later, such as boosting cancer patients' health. Carbs, which are believed to increase glucose and insulin, are restricted by the keto diet. It forces the body as fuel to burn fat. Any of the Fat is converted into ketones, which are used as another form of food for the brain and many other tissues. "In a statement, Barbara Gower, PhD, senior author and professor in the Department of Nutrition Sciences, said, "Since cancer cells tend to use glucose, diets that reduce glucose may be helpful." Because they limit glucose and several growth factors, the ability of cancer to grow will be limited by ketogenic diets, giving the patient's immune system time to respond."

The research states, "It may be difficult for keto dieters to meet their energy and protein requirements, and the diet may cause long-term problems, including kidney damage, higher levels of cholesterol, unintentional weight loss, bone loss, and certain vitamin and mineral deficiencies." They say a more balanced

approach to diet should be recommended, and cite evidence that it can help one's general well-being decrease processed carbs and increase the amount of healthy fats eaten.

16. Prevents And Reduces Migraines

A diet high in fats, mild in protein, and very poor in carbohydrates is ketogenic or ketogenic. For long time it has been used for the treatment of Epilepsy, a seizure-causing brain disease. The keto diet has been recommended to relieve or avoid other brain conditions such as migraine because of its therapeutic effects on the treatment of Epilepsy. Keto refers to a diet composed mainly of extremely low carbohydrate fats, usually less than 50 grams daily. The typical American adult absorbs 200-350 grams of carbohydrates every day, for comparison. In a variety of foods, such as bananas, breads, cereals, noodles, milk and other milk products, and starchy vegetables such as potatoes and maize, carbs are included. Your body usually breaks down carbohydrates into glucose from these foods to provide energy to your cells. Yet, for 3-4 days, when you seriously exclude carbohydrates from your diet, your body must search for new fuel sources to fulfill its energy needs.

It does so by breaking down fats in your liver to create ketones that can be quickly used for energy by your body and brain. When blood ketone levels increase above average, the body

enters a physiological state called ketosis. These ketones have been suggested to have defensive properties against migraine. Headaches that cause intense throbbing or pulsing pain, usually on one side of the head, are characterized by migraine. Other effects, such as nausea and sensitivity to light or sound, may follow this discomfort. Although the exact mechanism remains unknown, it is suspected that ketones created while on a keto diet restore brain excitability and energy metabolism in people with migraine to combat brain inflammation.

Chapter 3: How Safe Is Keto Diet?

In this chapter, we will give you a detailed view about how safe the keto diet is.

3.1. Keto Long- Term Effects

There's no one exactly sure. When the diet is maintained for up to one to two years or longer, most experiments have looked at the impact of KD in humans.

Longer-term experiments carried out on animals have demonstrated that certain adverse effects can be linked with KD. For example, in rat Findings, some will experience non-alcoholic fatty liver disease (defined as liver damage that is not due to excess alcohol intake, viral or autoimmune causes and iron overload) and insulin resistance. Other reports indicate that if they eat a very high-fat diet for a prolonged period, certain people might be predisposed to heart-related issues.

In several studies, especially among obese men and women, the keto diet is effective. Findings shows that KD can effectively assist in handling conditions such as:

- Obesity.

- Diabetes Type 2. Among type 2 diabetics, it can also minimize the need for drugs.

- Heart disease. It is difficult to relate the ketogenic diet to cardiovascular disease risk factors. Several studies have shown that keto diets may contribute to substantial reductions in overall cholesterol, rises in levels of HDL cholesterol, decreases in levels of triglycerides and decreases in levels of LDL cholesterol, as well as possible changes in levels of blood pressure.

- Neurological disorders, including Alzheimer's, dementia, multiple sclerosis and Parkinson's.

- Seizure symptoms and seizures.

- Polycystic ovarian syndrome (PCOS), among women of reproductive age, is the most prevalent endocrine condition.

- Certain forms of cancer, as cancers of the liver, colon, pancreas and ovaries.

- And others.

Is keto life safe? How long is safe for ketosis to be present? As mentioned above, Findings tells us that when pursued for about 2-6 months, or up to about two years or so when a specialist is supervising the person, the keto diet appears to be safest.

Keto Diet's Disadvantages (and Some Dangers)

1. Impact on the liver and kidneys

Some animal studies have shown that KD can lead to the accumulation of triglycerides and liver inflammation indicators, likely attributable to a higher dietary protein and fat content than other widely prescribed diets (such as the DASH diet or Mediterranean diet for example).

Investigators conclude that, by adopting low-carb, high-fat diets, genetics potentially play a part here, rendering certain persons more vulnerable to liver complications. For the kidneys, is the keto diet bad? "Patients with kidney disease need to be cautious because this diet could worsen their condition," according to a research published by Harvard Medical School.

2. May not lead to improved insulin sensitivity long-term

For people with diabetes, is the keto diet safe? The bulk of report suggests that yes, it is. However, while the KD may help decrease insulin resistance while somebody adheres to the diet rules and strictly controls their carb intake, these beneficial benefits may be short-lasting. Some animal experiments indicate that after carbohydrates are reintroduced back into the diet, insulin resistance/glucose intolerance may theoretically be improved.

However, other studies, especially among severely obese adults, indicate the opposite to be true. Therefore, Investigators note that the influence of the keto diet on glucose homeostasis remains controversial and relies on the prevalence of type 2 diabetes and genetic factors before beginning the diet.

3. Can cause side effects

It is not rare for people starting the keto diet to report signs of "keto flu," which may include: women's irritability, cravings, and menstrual problems, constipation, exhaustion, headaches, and decreased results of the exercise. These side effects are attributable to the body going through significant biochemical changes and removing from carbohydrates and sugar in essence.

In most cases, signs of keto flu resolve within a few weeks or even days, especially if someone eats a lot of whole foods, keeps reasonably active (such as walking, but does not start exercising at high intensity) and gets enough sleep.

4. Might be difficult to maintain weight loss

It is not immediately clear whether most people can sustain the weight loss gained on the keto diet until the diet stops, both because the diet can be difficult to adopt and because the body adapts metabolically. Long-term research on animals indicates

that after about six months on the diet, weight loss appears to plateau out, and can even start to climb back up.

The keto diet is not meant for long-term follow-up, which means that people prefer to find some way to achieve a balanced caloric consumption, such as carb-cycling or keto-cycling activities.

Final Thoughts: Is the Keto Diet Safe?

When it comes to the question "is it safe for the keto diet?" We need to take into account all short-term health changes associated with KD and uncertain possible long-term consequences. If they strictly observe the diet for more than about a year, certain persons appear to be genetically vulnerable to the ketogenic diet's harmful effects. Possible keto diet risks include: developing signs of short-term keto flu, struggling to sustain weight loss, failing to increase long-term insulin sensitivity, and potentially raising the possibility of complications with the liver, kidney or heart. While the ketogenic diet has some risks, the diet also encourages wellbeing in many ways. Ketogenic diet report papers demonstrate that obesity, type 2 diabetes, heart disease, epilepsy, strokes, PCOS, cancer and more can easily be reversed.

3.2. Keto Side Effects

The ketogenic diet, or keto diet, restricts carbs specifically while increasing the amount of fat individuals absorb. Keto flu, which involves fatigue, nausea, and headaches, is a frequent short-term side effect of the keto diet.

The long-term implications of observing the keto diet are not well established by investigators. For certain persons, though, it can cause health complications.

Keto flu

For certain persons, the keto diet is a dramatic improvement. More than half of the U.S. population consume at least the recommended number of whole grains per day, and about 70 percent eat more than the acceptable number of added sugars per day, according to the 2015–2020 Dietary Guidelines for Americans.

Consequently, for certain persons, a sudden transition to a low carbohydrate diet can cause side effects. People may suffer "keto flu" when transitioning into ketosis. Typical keto flu symptoms include:

- Insomnia

- Headaches

- Constipation

- Dizziness

- Fatigue

- Nausea And Vomiting

- Endurance Issues When Exercising

Keto flu is a short-term side effect for most persons that can recover over a matter of days or a few weeks. It can help to relieve the symptoms by drinking adequate fluids and electrolytes. An individual should talk to their doctor if they do not change.

Long-term health risks

Beyond the first 2 years, scientists do not know anything about the keto diet's long-term consequences. The possible dangers in any restrictive diet, though, include deficits in vitamins or minerals. An individual on a keto diet requires all possible outlets, including vegetables, fruits, and whole grains, to control carbohydrates' consumption. As a result, they will need to cut back on foods that have previously given them valuable nutrients. Lack in vitamins and minerals can cause a range of symptoms, ranging from mild to extreme. As a result of modifying their diet, a person adopting the keto diet would need to ensure that they do not lose out on any nutrients.

Additional possible dangers of a high fat, high protein diet include:

- Kidney stones

- Hypoproteinemia, or low-protein in the blood

- Hepatic steatosis (fatty liver)

In general, low carbohydrate diets might have harmful consequences. A 2016 report, for example, found that people with low carb diets have higher levels of low-density lipoprotein cholesterol, which is a heart disease risk factor.

Other considerations

There are several other drawbacks to the keto diet that a person might want to remember before attempting it, such as:

Varying outcomes: The keto diet may work more successfully for some people than others in weight loss. Based on many variables, according to the Academy of Nutrition and Dietetics, the rate at which individuals get into ketosis and start losing fat varies. The diet would also affect people differently.

Difficult to follow: The keto diet specifically controls what can be consumed by a human. As a result, for a prolonged time, it can be impossible to adopt the diet. If a person avoids limiting carbohydrates, whatever weight they have lost can be recovered.

Saturated fat: Because a person may stay in ketosis irrespective of the form of fat they eat, this may contribute to strong dependency on animal fats or saturated fats with long-term health risks.

People can reduce the keto diet's possible risks by:

- Making sure they get adequate vitamins and minerals from their diet

- Consuming better fats than saturated fats, such as olive oil, fatty fish and avocado

- Reduction of processed foods containing saturated fat

If weight reduction is their target, some carbs are slowly reintroduced until they achieve a moderate weight.

Who should try the keto diet?

For certain people to control their weight, the keto diet can be a successful way. Certain health problems can also enhance this eating habit. The National Centre for Health Findings, for example, states that dieting can help decrease the occurrence of convulsions in children with epilepsy, as well as regulate insulin levels and increase insulin sensitivity in people with diabetes. Though, people with any health problems should not observe the keto diet or should first discuss it with a doctor. Those

groups are those dealing with the following circumstances, according to the Academy of Nutrition and Dietetics:

- Pancreatic disease

- Gallbladder disease or removal

- A history of eating disorders

- Thyroid conditions

- Liver conditions

If a person wants to try the keto diet, they should consider talking to a certified dietician about their diet plan to decide if it is the best choice.

3.3. Keto Dawn Effects

What is the dawn effect?

The dawn effect applies, usually upon awakening, to an unexpected rise in fasting blood sugar. In the 1980s, doctors first noted it in patients with type 1 diabetes. Without the usual compensatory increase in insulin, they described the dawn effect as rising blood sugar. The body gradually raises glucose production as morning progresses. However, the patients, the night before took insufficient insulin to regulate the increase in glucose. The mismatch resulted in a rise in glucose in the blood.

The investigators determined that an uptick in the so-called "counter-regulatory hormones" cortisol, epinephrine, and norepinephrine triggered the early morning glucose spike. They are labeled counter-regulatory hormones mainly because the effects of insulin are "countered". These contra-regulatory hormones activate the liver to secrete glucose into the bloodstream. If a person has a normal insulin reaction, their insulin level increases to keep their blood glucose level steady. The excess glucose circulates until it is soaked up by the cells and used for energy for individuals witnessing the dawn effect. The body preparing itself for the additional energy needs required to wake up and to ensure that enough glucose is available for use every morning as a human becomes involved.

Studies in individuals without diabetes demonstrate that the body increases insulin secretion between 4 am and 8 am. This additional insulin boost stabilizes the rise in blood glucose levels from counter-regulatory hormones.

The dawn effect was thus considered, for decades, to be an issue only for people with type 1 or type 2 diabetes. But now, maybe the belief is shifting.

Implications

A prominent dawn effect for people with diabetes means an inability to control blood sugar in the morning and may have long-term health consequences. One analysis found that the dawn effect was associated with a rise in hemoglobin A1C (HbA1c) levels of 0.4 percent (4 mmol/mole), approximately representing the 3-month average blood sugar levels. The dawn effect is expected to have adverse health effects for people with diabetes because higher HbA1c levels associate with a higher risk of complications. To enhance optimal glucose regulation, the latest advice is to handle the dawn effect with drugs actively. So, what about people who are not diabetes sufferers? What if they follow a low-carb diet and burn fat for food instead of glucose preferentially? Will there be the same effects for the dawn effect? Next, we'll discuss that.

The dawn effect in Keto diet

The bad news comes first. For people who adopt a very Keto diet, we are not aware of any Findings trials that look at the dawn effect. However, the dawn effect is relatively normal for those adopting a rigid Keto diet based on clinical experience. Dream of physiology. Your body secretes counter-regulatory hormones as you get closer to awakening, increasing the liver's glucose production. But if blood glucose drops, it means there is no compensatory increase in insulin. Again, there is no concrete evidence to explain whether there is an uptick in blood

sugar, but hypotheses remain. One theory is that, because it rarely occurs on a very low-carb diet, the pancreas does not need to respond immediately to elevated blood sugar. The feedback loop rebalances, in turn. The emphasis of another hypothesis is on muscle cells. Muscle cells are the main cause of glucose absorption under glucose-burning conditions, pulling glucose out of the blood to use it for energy.

However, when the cells mainly burn fat for fuel instead, as they do when dietary carbohydrates are drastically decreased, glucose is not required by the muscle cells. In the other hand, the brain is also in need of some glucose. To make the brain "first in line" for usable glucose, muscle cells become "resistant" to glucose. Many call this metabolic phenomenon "adaptive glucose sparing" or "physiological insulin resistance." The concept is that, as it does in diabetes, the loss of glucose absorption exists for a positive cause, not a detrimental reason. This is a theory, but it is a theory that makes sense in terms of how the body functions. Some claim that insulin resistance provided our hunter-gatherer ancestors with an evolutionary advantage, helping their brains to use glucose and allowing their bodies to operate on fat.

The appearance or absence of elevated insulin levels may be one basic distinction between potentially dangerous and

possibly healthy elevated glucose. In an insulin resistance setting with elevated insulin levels, elevated glucose is expected to have a different biochemical outcome than the same glucose in an insulin sensitivity setting with low insulin level.

Is the dawn effect always harmful?

While findings indicate that the dawn effect is potentially dangerous to people with type 2 diabetes, can we say the same for those without diabetes?

It appears that blood glucose has adverse consequences in two forms. This is when glucose is chronically high, and the other is when there are significant changes or "spikes" of blood glucose levels, known as the variability of glucose. Studies suggest that both pathways accelerate vascular and endothelial disease. We could infer that there is no chronic elevation and the increase or spike is relatively minor. If none of these problems are present, there may be no vascular or other health effects. HbA1c does not account for shorter, more extreme blood sugar elevations, often referred to as glycemic heterogeneity. A rise in post-meal glucose to 140 mg/dL (7.8 mmol/L) is considered natural. We should also conclude that there should be no reason of concern for a dawn effect of up to 140 mg/dL (7.8 mmol/L). This could be particularly valid if the day's peak

blood sugar levels are in the morning, and the post-meal level is slightly lower during low-carb meals. But again, there is no knowledge about this, but it's a guess. It makes sense, though.

Based on this hypothesis, if dawn blood glucose levels do not reach 140 mg/dL (7.8mmol/L) and post-meal elevations are smaller than 140 mg/dL (7.8mmol/L) while HbA1c is in the normal range or rising, then it appears fair that the dawn effect is not a health issue. However, if these conditions are not met, the morning elevation can add to an ongoing problem and speed up vascular damage.

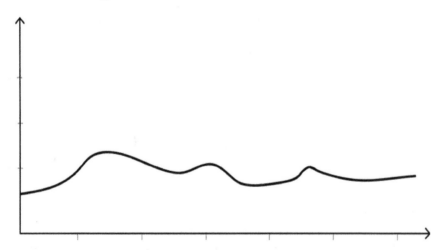

As an example, below represents a graph of a continuous glucose monitor (CGM) that will mean a better probability that the dawn effect would not have adverse health effects. Note that the peak dose of glucose is 120 mg/dL (6.7 mmol/L) which

is the maximum level of the day, with post-meal levels remaining below 110 mg/dL (6.1 mmol/L) and returning after an hour to baseline.

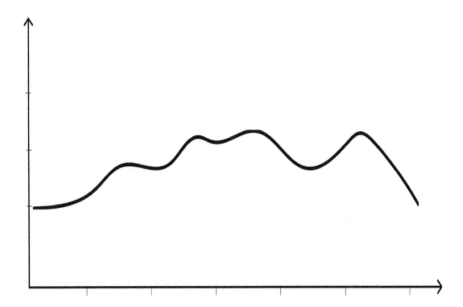

On the other hand, this graph indicates that the dawn effect is part of a broader problem. With a 130 mg/dL (7.2 mmol/L) peak, blood sugar starts high and never gets down to baseline until rising again after meals to just above 140 mg/dL (7.8 mmol/L).

In the following ways, these two graphs differ:

1. Degree of elevation of blood sugar

2. Chronic essence of elevation of blood sugar

3. The possible underlying reasons for the spike in blood sugar

Can you decrease the dawn effect?

The dawn impact may not be a problem for certain individuals. So, what would you do to minimize it if you believe it might lead adversely to your health?

- Exercise will improve. The degree and length of the glucose increase can be decreased by performing physical exertion after dinner and first thing upon waking.

- Eating early in the morning will also help to decrease the dawn effect. It can sound paradoxical, this guidance.

- Note, to ensure sufficient glucose levels, the dawn effect is triggered by lower-than-normal insulin secretion in the morning. If you eat food, it will inform your body that you have enough energy, and your insulin will react properly. The effect is enough insulin to help lower your level of glucose.

- Some individuals consider eating a low-carb, high-fat, or high-protein snack before bed to mitigate the dawn effect. This is not a perfect choice for those looking to profit from intermittent fasting. Yet that could be a safer alternative than beginning a medicine. Whether this advice is right for them should be decided by each person.

- In the morning, monitoring your blood glucose will inform you how it works with this technique.

- Don't forget about sleep's significance! A bad night's sleep can increase cortisol output, resulting in a more important dawn effect.

- Finally, the use of drugs may be considered by others. Taking insulin in the evening appears to be more effective at reducing the degree and length of glucose elevation than oral diabetes drugs.

There are possible side effects of all drugs, especially insulin, including the possibility of dangerously low blood sugar.

Chapter 4: Introduction of Ketosis

Ketosis is a normal metabolic condition. It involves the body making ketone bodies out of fat and using them instead of carbs for energy. By adopting a very low carb, high-fat ketogenic diet, you will get into ketosis. A ketogenic diet will help you lose weight. You will easily lose weight in the short term, and it reduces the body's reserves of glycogen and water.

It will suppress your appetite in the long run, leading to a lower intake of calories. Ketosis can have some health effects, such as fewer seizures in children with epilepsy and leading to weight loss.

4.1. What is ketosis?

Ketosis is a metabolic condition in which ketones in the blood have a high concentration. This occurs because much of the body's food is provided by fat, and there is minimal access to glucose. For several cells of the body, glucose (blood sugar) is the preferred fuel supply. Very commonly, ketosis is related to ketogenic and very low carb diets. It also occurs during breastfeeding, childbirth, fasting, and hunger. To get started with ketosis, you normally need to consume less than 50 grams of carbohydrates a day and occasionally as little as 20 grams a

day. The exact carb intake that will cause ketosis, however, varies between people.

You may need to exclude those food products from your diet to do this, such as:

- Grains

- Candy

- Sugary soft drinks

You also have:

- Legumes

- Potatoes

- Fruit

The hormone insulin levels go down by eating a very low carb diet and fatty acids are released significantly from body fat reserves. Many of these fatty acids are taken into the liver, oxidized and converted into ketones (or ketone bodies). These molecules can provide the body with energy. Ketones can cross the blood-brain barrier to supply energy for the brain in the absence of glucose, unlike fatty acids.

Ketones can supply energy for the brain

It's a common misconception that the brain doesn't work

without dietary carbohydrates. It's true that glucose is favored and that only glucose for food can be used by certain cells in the brain.

However, a significant portion of your brain will also use ketones for nutrition, such as through hunger or when your diet is low in carbohydrates. Currently, the brain receives 25 percent of its nutrition from ketones after just three days of malnutrition. This number increases to about 60 percent during long-term hunger. Besides, to generate the glucose the brain still needs during ketosis, your body can use protein or other molecules. Gluconeogenesis is called this phase. Ketosis and gluconeogenesis are completely capable of satisfying the energy requirements of the brain.

Ketosis is not the same as ketoacidosis

People sometimes misinterpret ketosis and ketoacidosis for each other. Although ketosis is part of natural metabolism, ketoacidosis is a harmful metabolic disorder that can be lethal if left unchecked. The body is saturated with exceptionally high levels of glucose (blood sugar) and ketones during ketoacidosis. The blood turns acidic as this occurs, which is severely dangerous. Ketoacidosis is generally associated with type 1 diabetes, which is not regulated. In persons with type 2 diabetes, it can also occur, but this is less common.

Furthermore, serious abuse of alcohol may contribute to ketoacidosis.

Effects on epilepsy

A neurological disease characterized by frequent seizures is epilepsy. It is a neurological disorder that is extremely widespread, affecting about 70 million people worldwide. To better treat seizures, most patients with epilepsy take anti-seizure drugs. Despite taking these drugs, however, about 30 percent of persons appear to have seizures. The ketogenic diet was elaborated in the early 1920s as a cure for seizures in patients who did not respond to drug treatment. It has been used mainly in infants, with effects seen in some Findings. Although following a ketogenic diet, many kids with epilepsy have seen substantial declines in seizures, and some have seen complete recovery.

Effects on weight loss

A common weight loss diet is the ketogenic diet, and Findings has shown it can be effective. Any studies have found that ketogenic diets are more useful than low-fat diets for weight loss. Compared to those on a reduced-fat, calorie-restricted diet, one report recorded 2.2 times more weight loss for persons on a ketogenic diet. It is generally accepted, however, that sticking

to a diet is important for long-term success. The ketogenic diet can be simple for some people to stick to, while others may find it unhealthy.

Any studies show that the keto diet might not be the most successful way to lose weight. The authors of a 2019 report found that helping people lose weight was not safer than other diets, and it could not have unique benefits for people with metabolic disorders.

4.2. What Are Ketones?

It's important to grasp ketones before digging into the ins and outs of ketosis. There are three kinds of bodies of ketones:

- Acetoacetate

- Beta-Hydroxybutyrate (BHB)

- Acetone

The first ketone produced from breaking down fat is acetoacetate. This then contributes to the production of the most concentrated ketone in the human body, beta-hydroxybutyrate. Finally, acetone is spontaneously generated through decarboxylation as a side product of acetoacetate.

Why Your Body Uses Ketones

From an evolutionary standpoint, while glucose supplies

became limited, humans still depended on ketones for nutrition (i.e., no fruits available during winter). Your ancestors undoubtedly had regular periods where there was not immediately available elevated carb-heavy food. For this cause, the human body is still able to respond to fuel-burning ketones.

Ketosis is a normal physiological condition, and most infants are born in a state of ketosis. However, individuals join ketosis with the plentiful supplies of carbohydrates available today, and it becomes a latent metabolic pathway. The keto diet object is to remove carbohydrates deliberately, thereby pressuring the body to turn to an alternate food source.

4.3. Benefits of Ketosis

For all, ideal diet is different; there is no one-size-fits-all solution. That said, a ketogenic diet focused on whole food gives most people a variety of benefits, including reduced body fat, increased insulin sensitivity, and improved mental and physical health.

Certain medical disorders, including asthma, Alzheimer's disease, depression, cancer, heart disease, and migraines, have also been found to help prevent or enhance ketosis.

Weight Loss Benefits of Ketosis

For the following factors, ketosis may be a beneficial path to weight loss:

- **Increased fat oxidation:** In ketosis, as its main fuel supply, the body burns dietary fat and your body fat.

- **Regulation of hormones:** By manipulating hormones that affect weight, ketosis can help sustain weight loss. This means that a keto diet will help prevent cravings for fatty foods, decreasing the risk of regaining weight.

- **Appetite suppression:** Feeling whole, even on a diet for weight loss, means you can better listen to the true signs of appetite from your body.

- **Regulation of blood sugar:** Weight loss diets that contain high carbohydrates will cause blood sugar spikes that soon after eating leave you feeling hungry again and exhausted and unfocused. You may feel healthy insulin levels on the keto diet, which will thus avoid blood sugar spikes.

Exercise Benefits of Ketosis

- During exercise, ketosis can be helpful through:

- Increase and prolong your rate of stamina.

- Adjusting the body to burn more fat, which helps to conserve muscle glycogen.

- Improving the function of mitochondria, enzymes and fat use to enhance long-term optimal health and physical fitness.

- More effective use of oxygen, which results in improved outcomes for endurance athletes.

Mental Focus Benefits of Ketosis

An unbalanced diet will lead to a loss of mental clarity, posing as a foggy head, finding crucial details difficult to recall, or failing to remain focused on tasks. Ketones increase mitochondrial production and energy levels, which provide energy for cells in your body and brain. It is important to eat healthy fats. In your body, every single cell requires fat to work, especially your brain cells. The brain, which consists of over 60 percent fat and likes fat for food, is the fattiest organ.

4.4. Ketosis Health Benefits

Here are 10 proven health advantages to diets that are low-carb and ketogenic.

1. Reduce your hunger Low-carb diets

The worst side effect of dieting appears to be thirst. That is one

of the key reasons that many individuals feel miserable and giving up ultimately. A low-carb diet, however, leads to an involuntary appetite loss. Studies repeatedly demonstrate that they wind up eating much less calories as people cut sugars and consume more protein and fat.

2. Low-carb diets tend at first to further loss of weight

One of the easiest and most effective ways to reduce weight is to cut carbohydrates. Studies suggest that individuals shed more weight sooner on low-carb diets than those on low-fat diets, even though the latter deliberately limits calories. In the first week or two, low-carb diets work to get rid of extra water from the body, reduce insulin levels and lead to accelerated weight loss.

3. From the stomach cavity comes a larger proportion of fat loss.

Subcutaneous fat, which is beneath the clothing, and visceral fat, which accumulates in the stomach cavity common for most overweight men, are the two major forms. They appear to lodge visceral fat around the lungs. Inflammation and insulin resistance are associated with excess visceral fat and can drive the metabolic syndrome so prevalent today in the West. To reduce this unhealthy abdominal fat, low-carb diets are very

successful. The abdominal cavity tends to come from a larger proportion of the weight people lose on low-carb diets. Over time, it can translate to a significantly lowered risk of heart failure and type 2 diabetes.

4. Tendency to decrease triglycerides Dramatically

Triglycerides are fat compounds that circulate in the bloodstream. High fasting triglycerides, levels in the blood after an overnight fast, are well known to be a strong risk factor for heart disease. Carb intake is one of the main drivers of elevated triglycerides in sedentary people, particularly simple sugar fructose. They appear to undergo a very drastic drop in blood triglycerides as people remove carbs. Low-fat diets, on the other hand, also lead triglycerides to grow.

5. Increased 'Good' HDL Cholesterol levels

The 'healthy' cholesterol is also called high-density lipoprotein (HDL). The higher your HDL levels compared to "bad" LDL, the lower your heart disease risk.

One of the easiest ways to boost "good" HDL levels is eating fat, and low-carb diets contain many fat. It is also unsurprising that HDL levels rise significantly on balanced, low-carb diets, whereas on low-fat diets, they appear to increase only moderately or even decrease.

6. Reduced levels of Blood Sugar and Insulin

Globally, millions of individuals are affected by diabetes and insulin resistance, for these people, low-carb and ketogenic diets may also be especially effective. Studies suggest that reducing carbohydrates significantly reduces both blood sugar and insulin levels.

7. Can Reduce blood pressure

A major risk factor for many illnesses, including heart attack, stroke and kidney failure, is high blood pressure or hypertension. Low-carb diets are an efficient way to lower blood pressure, helping you survive longer and reduce the risk of these diseases.

8. Successful against metabolic syndrome

Metabolic syndrome is a disorder that is closely linked to the risk of heart failure and diabetes. Metabolic syndrome, in particular, is a series of symptoms, including:

- Stomach obesity

- High blood pressure

- High levels of fasting blood sugar

- Elevated triglycerides

- "Low levels of HDL cholesterol."

However, in treating all five of these symptoms, a low-carb diet is extremely successful. These symptoms are almost abolished on such a diet.

9. Improved levels of 'Poor' LDL Cholesterol

It is also more likely that people who have high "bad" LDL would have heart attacks. The size of the particles is, however, significant. A greater risk of heart attack is associated with smaller particles, whereas larger particles are associated with a lower risk. Low-carb diets, it points out, maximize the size of "bad" LDL particles while reducing overall LDL particles' volume in the bloodstream. As such, decreasing your carb intake will improve the well-being of your heart.

10. Preventive For multiple brain defects,

Your brain requires glucose, since only this form of sugar can be burnt in certain areas of it. That's why, if you don't eat any carbohydrates, the liver makes glucose from protein. Yet, ketones produced through starvation or carb intake are very limited and can also burn a significant portion of your brain. This is how the ketogenic diet works, this mechanism has been used for decades in children who do not respond to drug therapy to cure epilepsy.

4.5. Types Of Ketosis

A ketogenic diet is a diet intended to induce ketosis, break down body fat into ketones, and allow the body to operate on ketones rather than glucose to a large degree. There are various ways ketosis can be induced, so there are several ketogenic diet variations.

Since samen is the ultimate aim of these diets, there are typically various parallels between the various forms of ketogenic diet, especially in terms of being low in carbohydrates and high in dietary fat.

1. Standard Ketogenic Diet (SKD)

It is a very low carb diet, a mild protein diet and high fat. Usually, it contains 70 to 75% fat, 20% protein, and only 5 to 10% carbohydrates.

A traditional standard ketogenic diet, in terms of grams per day, will be:

- 20-50g of carbohydrate

- 40-60g of protein

- No set limit for fat

2. Very-low-carb ketogenic diet (VLCKD)

Very-low-carb is a traditional ketogenic diet, and so a VLCKD

would normally refer to a standard ketogenic diet.

3. Well Formulated Ketogenic Diet (WFKD)

The word 'Well Formulated Ketogenic Diet' comes from one of the leading ketogenic diet experts, Steve Phinney. As a traditional ketogenic diet, the WFKD follows a similar blueprint. Well formulated ensures that weight, protein, and carbohydrate macronutrients conform to the traditional ketogenic diet ratios and therefore have the greatest chance of ketosis happening.

4. MCT Ketogenic Diet

This follows the traditional ketogenic diet outline but insists on supplying more of the diet's fat content using medium-chain triglycerides (MCTs). MCTs are present in coconut oil and are available in the liquid form of MCT oil and MCT emulsion.

To treat epilepsy, MCT ketogenic diets have been used since the idea is that MCTs enable individuals to absorb more carbohydrates and proteins thus retaining ketosis. MCTs produce more ketones per gram of fat than the long-chain triglycerides found in natural dietary fat.

5. Calorie-restricted ketogenic diet

Except that calories are reduced to a fixed number, a calorie-

restricted ketogenic diet is identical to a normal ketogenic diet. Findings indicate that whether calorie consumption is reduced or not, ketogenic diets appear to be efficient. This is because it helps to avoid over-eating in itself from the satiating effect of eating fat and being in ketosis.

6. Cyclical Ketogenic Diet (CKD)

Often known as carb backloading, the CKD diet contains days on which more carbohydrates are ingested, such as five ketogenic days accompanied by two higher carb days. The diet is meant for athletes who can replenish glycogen removed from muscles during workouts using the higher carb days.

7. Targeted Ketogenic Diet (TKD)

Except that carbohydrates are eaten around exercise hours, the TKD is close to a traditional ketogenic diet. It is a combination between a regular ketogenic diet and a cyclical ketogenic diet that requires every day you exercise to eat carbohydrates. It is focused on the assumption that carbohydrates eaten before or during a physical effort can be absorbed even more effectively, while the need for energy from the muscles rises while we are involved.

8. High Protein Ketogenic Diet

With a 35 percent protein ratio, 60 percent fat, and 5 percent

carbohydrates, this diet contains more protein than a regular ketogenic diet. Data shows that a high-protein ketogenic is useful for weight loss in people who need to lose weight. As for other types of ketogenic diet, there is a lack of evidence about whether there are any health hazards if practiced for several years.

Chapter 5: Keto and weight loss

In this chapter, we will focus on Keto diet and weight loss.

How to Lose Weight with the Keto Diet

For certain individuals, ketogenic dieting is a major leap. You're transitioning to a different biochemical substrate. It may take some getting used to that. The easiest way to increase the odds of success is to get at least a few weeks of a primal-aligned eating routine in place. (The Keto Reset Diet establishes a step-by-step protocol to do this in 21 days. Mark's Everyday Apple is all about the transformation and maintenance of Primal feeding. If you're new to the site, I'd urge you to start here.)

Make a Minimum Commitment to Six Weeks

When you move to new fuel sources, the first three weeks can be the most complicated, but you can expect breakthroughs. (In the early weeks, certain extreme athletes will undergo a brief performance decline, but they can rebound strongly after 4 weeks and beyond.) When you get to the six-week point, the metabolic machinery is in place, and the adaptation is impossible to undo. Extra mitochondria don't just vanish.

Get Plenty of Electrolytes

Lots of sodium, magnesium, and potassium are what you'll

require. On top of the usual diet, try 4.5 grams of sodium (about 2 teaspoons of fine salt or a little less than 3 teaspoons of kosher salt), 300-400 mg of magnesium and 1-2 grams of potassium per day. Going keto flushes out the weight of liquids, and with that, lots of electrolytes leave.

Eat large, but don't be crazy about it

Only because a high-fat diet is a ketogenic diet does not mean you have to consume ungodly levels of fat. It's all of not consuming carbs than eating as much fat as possible to be ketogenic. Eating additional fat in the first 4-7 days can speed up keto-adaptation (increasing AMPK signaling). You should get your diet down to the recommended 65-75 percent of overall caloric intake in the first week.

Take The Vegetables

Keto-friendly is the overwhelming bulk of vegetables. They not only supply essential micronutrients and phytonutrients, but they also supply negligible quantities of carbohydrates. Over-ground vegetables should be the bulk of your keto diet in terms of volume to fulfill your critical micronutrient requirements, even though fat will supply the rest of your calories.

Eat the Berries

The glycemic load of raspberries, blackberries, strawberries,

and blueberries is minimal, and the phytonutrients are exceptionally large. Although consuming a flat of strawberries is not very ketogenic, you won't be knocked out by a huge bowlful.

Eat fiber

Many individuals appear to neglect or malign fiber on ketogenic diets. It is an error. Fiber does not digest into glucose first. Second, fiber feeds the gut biome, providing your gut bacteria with fermentable substrate to turn them into helpful short-chain fatty acids and support your immune system.

Lift Heavy Stuff

The fact that they induce loss of lean mass is a frequent critique of ketogenic diets. That's not baseless. If your ketogenic diet decreases your appetite so much that you lose weight when feeding, you will lose muscle. You could lose muscle if you are on a super-low-protein ketogenic diet. By transmitting an anabolic signal to your muscles and allowing more protein intake without hampering ketosis, lifting weights avoids these problems.

Do a lot of physical exercise at a low level

Running, climbing, jogging, swimming, rowing. Keep it in the aerobic HR region (heartbeats per minute below 180 minus

age) and you can increase your body fat utilization, which will speed up ketone development and adaptation.

Don't forget to sign up for our keto-themed update, the Keto Reset Digest. You get:

- Unpublished unique commentary on fresh Findings, patterns, conversations and perspectives on the ketogenic diet

- The best keto news and analysis curated

- Appetizing keto dishes that are nourishing

- 20 percent off any keto items in the Keto Range Primal Kitchen®

5.1. Low Carbohydrate Diets

How much carbohydrates ought to be removed on a keto diet? How much carbohydrates would you consume? Depending on you as a person and your priorities, the response depends a little.

The lower the calories, the greater the effect on weight loss and the decline in cravings and appetite. The less calories you consume, the better your blood glucose and insulin tolerance will increase if you have type 2 diabetes. However, others find a very low carb diet too restricting and difficult.

Here are three examples, based on how many carbohydrates you eat a day, of how a low-carb dinner can look.

Ketogenic

Under 20 grams per day

Moderate

20-50 grams per day

Liberal

50-100 grams per day.

For certain people, the plate on the left will be keto-genic. Although very healthy, the other two would not possibly be ketogenic, but may also lead to progressive weight loss and increased blood glucose and insulin sensitivity. Low carb is

described as something under 100 grams per day. Remember that there are sometimes 250 grams of carbohydrates a day on a Western diet, or even more.

How we define low carb and keto

We describe the various levels of carbohydrates this way:

Low carb keto: less than 20 grams of carbohydrates a day. For certain individuals, this amount will be ketogenic.

Less than 4 percent of the overall nutrition in our keto recipes comes from sugars, and the remainder comes from protein and fat. We also keep the amount of protein in keto recipes moderate. Some can find that protein is sufficiently transformed into glucose above this range to increase blood sugar levels—moderate low carb content: 20 to 50 grams a day. Energy extracted from carbohydrates would range about 4 and 10 percent in our relatively low carb recipes. The majority will come from fat and protein.

Liberal low carb: 50 to 100 grams a day. Energy extracted from carbohydrates would be 10 to 20 percent energy in our liberal low-carb recipes. The majority will come from fat and protein.

What is protein?

Many smaller units, called amino acids, are made up of protein. Although your body will produce most of the 20 amino acids it wants, there are nine that it cannot make. This are referred to as essential amino acids and must be ingested regularly in food. Since animal foods contain nearly the same quantities of all 9 essential amino acids, they are called 'full' proteins. On the other hand, almost all plants lack one or two essential amino acids and are known as "incomplete" proteins. Animal protein products that are keto-friendly include beef, fish, seafood, eggs and cheese. Tofu and soy-based products and most nuts and seeds contain keto-friendly plant protein sources, although some are higher in carbs than others.

What does protein do in your body?

In your body, protein is a main component of any cell. It is broken down into individual amino acids when you ingest protein, which is absorbed into your muscles and other tissues.

There are only a handful of the major roles of proteins:

- Muscle repair and growth. The protein in your muscles is usually broken down and reconstructed daily, and for muscle protein synthesis, new muscle development, a fresh supply of amino acids is needed. Eating enough dietary protein helps to reduce muscle deterioration and stimulates muscle development when combined with strength exercise.

- Keeping the skin, hair, nails, and bones as well as our internal organs safe. While protein turnover happens more slowly in these structures than in the muscle, new amino acids are needed to replace old and degraded ones over time.

- Hormone and enzyme formation. Many of the hormones required for life are also proteins, like insulin and growth hormone. Similarly, most enzymes are proteins in the human body. To produce these essential molecules, the body relies on a continuous supply of amino acids.

Furthermore, both professional experience and findings show that it will help make weight loss easier to have adequate protein. This may be because, by activating hormones that encourage feelings of fullness and happiness, protein will suppress hunger and avoid overeating.

For each meal, target at least 20 grams of protein

To ensure that amino acids are absorbed into your bodies,

report has proposed that your body requires between 20-30 grams of protein at any meal. Therefore, rather than eating more of it at one meal, it might be better to divide your protein consumption equally over two or three feedings, at least if you want to maximize your muscle mass. It did not improve instant muscle development by adding more to a meal. Some have taken this to mean that "wasted" was over 30 grams in a single meal. This is not what the studies revealed, however.

Older people and children have increased protein requirements. Growing children have a higher protein RDA than adults (0.95g/kg vs. 0.8g/kg), which makes scientific sense with the higher growth rate. When we become young adults, our protein requirements relative to our height and body weight are not as high as those of infants. But as we reach old age, our desires rise again.

Training in resistance increases the protein needs. People who participate in weightlifting, other types of strength training, and fitness of the endurance probably require more protein than sedentary people of the same height and weight. Aim for a protein intake at or near the top of your range when you do strength training, particularly if your goal is to build muscle. A total protein consumption of up to approximately 1.6 g/kg/day may help increase muscle mass. However, bear in

mind that there is a limit on how easily you can raise muscle mass, regardless of how much protein you eat, even with intensive exercise.

Every day, how much protein do I eat?

Having the right amount of protein needn't be difficult or frustrating. You will end up inside your goal range much of the time by merely consuming a quantity that is satisfying and paying attention to when you start feeling whole.

To get 20-25 grams of protein, here are the quantities of food you need to eat:

- 100 grams of beef, poultry or fish (3.5 ounces) (about the size of a deck of cards)

- 4 large eggs

- 240 grams of pure Greek yogurt (8 ounces)

- 210 grams of cottage cheese (7 ounces)

- 100 grams of hard cheese (3.5 ounces) (about the size of a fist)

- 100 grams of almonds, peanuts or pumpkin seeds (3.5 ounces) (about the size of a fist)

A limited amount of protein, about 2-6 grams per average meal, is given by other nuts, seeds, and vegetables.

5.3. Keto Food For Weight Loss

Below is the full weight loss list of Ketogenic Diet Foods:

1. Oils and Fats

The body needs fats, too much of it, especially if you get them from the wrong sources, can be harmful. You can eat several ways in a ketogenic diet, although this should not make it complicated since most diets are normally a mixture of various types of fats. A summary to give you a better understanding is below.

• Trans Fats. Stop this to the fullest degree possible. There are hydrogenated fats that have been processed chemically to extend certain foods' shelf life. Margarine is an example of a diet rich in Trans fats, which can cause heart attacks if too much is eaten.

• Polyunsaturated Fats. There are two kinds of these: the normal and the refined. Margarine spreads contain refined polyunsaturated fats, whereas natural polyunsaturated fats are extracted from fatty fish and animal protein.

• Monounsaturated Fats. These can be found in macadamia nuts, mango, and olives.

• Saturated Fats. These can be contained in lard, coconut oil, ghee, and butter.

Below are some food choices rich in oils and fats that are beneficial to the ketogenic diet:

- Cocoa butter

- Avocados

- Tallow

- Lard

- Non-hydrogenated animal fat

- MCT oil

- Macadamia oil

- Avocado oil

- Coconut oil

- Coconut butter

- Mayonnaise

- Ghee/ Butter

- Brazil/Macadamia nuts

- Egg yolks

- Olive oil

- Fatty fish

Always go for cold-pressed oils such as safflower, soybean, flax, or olive when it comes to vegetable oils.

2. Keto Protein Foods List

Some protein-rich food options helpful to the ketogenic diet are below:

- Eggs. Wild game, pheasant, quail, duck, goose, among others.

- Bacon. When purchasing ham, pork chops, pork loin, tenderloin, and ground pork, select fattier cuts. Beware with added sugars.

- Beef. Again, when purchasing stew pork, roasts, steak, and ground beef, select fattier cuts.

- Whole Shells. Your local store should have free-range eggs. Be it scrambled, poached, grilled, devilled, or fried, cook them in every way that you can.

- Shellfish. Pork chops, pork loin, Squid, crab, lobster, clams, and oysters.

- Fishes. The fattier the fish, the better the keto diet would be. Tuna, trout, snapper, flounder, salmon, mahi-mahi, mackerel, cod, catfish, and other wild-caught fish are your options.

- Organ/Offal. Offal is high in vitamins and minerals, including the tongue, intestine, liver, and heart.

- Other Meat. Fattier cuts are also applicable. Turkeys, lambs, pigs, and veal's are your options.

- Bacon and sausage. For extra fillers and those cured in butter, stop everything. Nitrates need not to be a concern.

- Nut Butter. As they are rich in omega 6s, be careful of legumes, but feast on unsweetened nuts high in calories, such as macadamia nut butter and almond butter.

3. Keto-Friendly Fruits and Vegetables

A significant part of the keto diet is fruits and vegetables, but

beware of those varieties that are rich in sugar. To not make the error of sacrificing your diet, you should be able to recognize them.

Make sure you have the required quantity of:

- Citrus Fruits: Black, lime, and lemon are used in these.

- Berries: They are all healthy, whether they are blackberries, blueberries, or raspberries.

- Nightshades: Eat a healthy number of onions, onions, and eggplants.

You should also eat high-carbohydrate vegetables, just make sure you limit your consumption. Squash, garlic, mushrooms, parsnip and onion are your choices. You can, meanwhile, keep away from immense fruits and starchy vegetables such as bananas and potatoes.

4. Keto Dairy

Those who have difficulty eating dairy products, because they contain less lactose, go for long-age and very hard dairy products. There are some examples:

- Alternatives to mayonnaise and mayo

- Hard cheeses include Swiss, feta, parmesan and aged cheddar cheese

- Monterey Jack, Colby, blue, brie, and mild mozzarella cheese

- Spreadable goods such as cream cheese, mascarpone, cream cheese, sour cream, and cottage cheese

- Heavy whipped cream

- Greek yogurt.

5. Keto Seeds and Nuts

A lot of people use raw nuts to add texture or boost their meals' taste. Some still love to binge on them, which may be enjoyable but does not relate precisely to weight loss objectives. Snacking would likely only increase the body's insulin levels, which slows down the rate of weight loss.

At least pick some that are helpful to the keto diet if you're craving nuts, such as:

- Walnuts

- Cashews

- Pistachios

- Pine nuts

- Hazelnuts

- Almonds

- Pecans

- Brazil nuts

- Macadamia nuts

Remember to eat liberally, since nuts contain carbohydrates. Certain nuts, including cashews and pistachios, are naturally rich in them. Instead, you should eat sunflower seed flour as a supplement for almond flour if you are allergic to nuts and try to keep an eye out for omega-6 fatty acids.

6. Keto Drinks

Drink lots of fluids to replenish your electrolytes, since they are not limited to water alone, which should be simple. Once in a while, you should also drink sporting juices and bone broth.

When it comes to Keto diet-friendly drinks, you have a lot of options, such as:

- Water. Your main hydration source. Hold a bottle close to you at all times and still reload, refill and refill.

- Tea. Not just for some tea. Choose black tea or green tea.

- Coffee. Coffee is high in antioxidants, has some advantages for weight loss, and increases mental concentration.

- Broth. Broth replenishes the electrolytes effortlessly. It's all high in minerals and vitamins and tastes fantastic to boot.

- Almond or Coconut Milk. Replace almond milk or coconut milk for your milk product, just make sure to choose the supermarket's unsweetened variety.

Once in a while, you should drink alcohol too, but maybe get rid of wine and beer and prefer hard liquor. Alcohol and wine are also rich in sugars, so stop them at all times if you do not want to add further weight.

5.4. Keto With Intermittent Fasting

What is Intermittent Fasting?

Intermittent fasting applies, in simplistic words, to a shortened meal frequency. Although there are many IF variants, a once-weekly 24 hour fast, alternate day fasting (ADF) or a 5:2 fast are the most common types, including fasting 2 consecutive days out of every week. The "intermittent" aspect of IF means you do not fast regularly.

That is what distinguishes IF from time-limited eating (TRF). The tradition of reducing your feeding window from 4 to 10 hours during the day to wherever, and fasting the rest of the time, is TRF. Most persons who pursue TRF do so every day, in comparison to IF.

The Science of IF

A metabolic reaction is activated every time we feed. If the meal includes carbohydrates, a rise in blood glucose (in different degrees) and insulin will be part of this metabolic reaction. To promote the uptake of blood glucose into our skeletal muscles, the pancreas releases insulin.

When insulin is released, it signals that the body retains extra energy as glycogen or adipose tissue. The liver and skeletal muscle are the main storage areas. Along with controlling energy storage processes, insulin inhibits others, particularly those that release fat from our stored deposits of adipose tissue.

There are many benefits, both physiological and psychological, of intermittent fasting.

For those trying to lose weight, the first advantage might be. While the evidence on this is not conclusive, many individuals say that it is far better to adhere to than conventional diets, which you are expected to eat far less calories than you need.

Some may find it easier to not consume than to keep calorie consumption well below their means chronically. This could be a neurological influence rather than the actual. Furthermore, IF

can make it easier to prepare meals (or not plan...if you catch our drift). You don't have to think about cooking a meal, finding time to feed, or thinking about what you're going to eat if today is one of your fasting days. This could unlock some time to be active at work or in hobbies when done correctly.

As far as science goes, intermittent fasting is in its infancy, and several trials have been done in rodents.

Lean and Mean

Body composition can benefit from IF. Fasting for 24 hours in humans can decrease weight and retain weight loss for up to 48 hours (most is probably just water weight). Multiple fasting periods (e.g. weekly 24-hour fasts) could, however, lead to long-term weight loss. Among people, this needs to be further discussed. In mice, the amount of visceral fat in these animals was dramatically decreased by a diet that mimicked fasting and replicated twice per month; with the added benefits of enhanced neurogenesis, better cognitive efficiency, and strengthened immune system.

Prosper and Live Healthy

It's difficult to Findings human longevity, so we don't have a lot of IF evidence supporting a longer life in this field. However, in rat models, relative to mice fed more regularly,

animals were fasted intermittently and displayed improved lifetime and health. Several pathways including increased autophagy, decreased oxidative stress, and lower insulin levels and insulin-like growth factor 1 could improve lifespan (IGF-1).

Metabolic stimulus

Through IF, some facets of metabolism and digestive health may be improved. Several risk factors for cardiovascular and cardiac disease have been found to decrease prolonged fasting levels, including: blood lipids (cholesterol and triglycerides), blood glucose, insulin, blood pressure, and inflammation. These metabolic advantages could come from the effects of fasting on regulating our circadian rhythms, sleep, and the gut's microbiome.

Individuals who report regular practice, intermittent fasting (i.e. IF) have a lower risk of diabetes, lowered blood glucose levels, and a lower body mass index. This indicates that fasting can help prevent many metabolic diseases from beginning. Fasting, however, may also counteract facets of conditions such as type 2 diabetes. This may include reducing glucose and insulin or improving immunity to insulin.

Chapter 6: Helpful Tips To Avoid Common Mistakes

In this chapter we will discuss about the helpful tips to avoid mistakes.

6.1. Keto On A Budget

We are proud to note that this keto has been used with tremendous results by thousands of people on a budget meal schedule! We have learned from the reviews we got and would like to advise how this keto diet strategy for beginners can make the most of it.

- On a budget meal schedule, measure the macros before beginning the keto. It's hard to make a meal schedule perfect for everyone, just make sure you match the macros delivered in this plan.

- This package contains 1200 calories a day. That is what most consumers are going to need at the low end. You can scale this up very quickly if you consume more than 1200 calories a day!

- This diet contains slightly more protein than most individuals that proceed with keto would require. By adding additional fat to foods, the best way to combat this is. It can give you a 1450 calorie plan with a very strong fat: protein ratio by adding 2 tablespoons of healthy fats per day.

If 1 meal planning is not enough for you, we have a complete 50-day plan that hundreds have used to lose weight effectively on a keto diet.

6.2. Keto Grocery List

The ingredients that make up the keto novice's shopping basket for our go-to keto recipes are listed below. To cook up your recipes at home, we suggest doubling up on the produce and proteins!

Produce

Ingredients

- Mushrooms

- Green onions

- White onion

- Red bell pepper

- Spinach

- Romaine or leaf lettuce

- Garlic

- Green cabbage

- Cherry tomatoes

- Avocado

- Lime

Proteins

Ingredients

- Boneless, skinless chicken breasts

- Breakfast sausage

- Bacon

- Ground beef

Eggs and dairy

Ingredients

- Cream cheese

- Plain, whole-milk yogurt

- Eggs

- Blue cheese

- Salted butter

Pantry staples

Ingredients

- Almond flour
- Soy sauce
- Vanilla extract
- Cocoa powder
- Monk fruit extract
- Almond butter
- Chicken broth
- Coconut cream

Spices and oils

- Garlic powder
- Coconut oil
- Sesame oil
- Sesame seeds
- Avocado oil
- Salt
- Pepper
- Ground ginger
- Cinnamon

6.3. Storage Guideline

Time limitations for Storage:

The following list shows how long you can store refrigerated foods, their freshness, and flavor and nutrient levels, to maintain their best quality. Food quality is also related to time limits for beef, poultry and fish.

- **Milk:** 7 days after "best before" date, opened or unopened

- **Yogurt:** 7 to 10 days, opened or unopened

- **Cheese, hard:** 3 to 4 weeks opened, 6 months unopened

- **Butter:** 4 weeks after best before date, opened or unopened

- **Eggs, in shell:** 4 weeks

- **Eggs, hard-cooked:** 1 week

- **Fresh meat:** 2 to 4 days

- **Fresh ground meat:** 1 to 2 days

- **Deli meats:** 3 to 4 days

- **Fresh chicken or turkey, whole or pieces:** 2 to 3 days

- **Fresh ground poultry:** 1 to 2 days

- **Cooked chicken:** 3 to 4 days

- **Fresh fish:** 2 to 3 days

- **Fresh shellfish:** 12 to 24 hours

- **Leftover soups, stews, casseroles:** 3 to 4 days

- **Jams and jellies:** 3 to 4 months, opened

- **Mayonnaise:** 2 to 3 months, opened

- **Mustard:** 1 year, opened

- **Ketchup:** 6 months, opened

- **Salad dressing or vinaigrette, bottled:** 6 to 9 months, opened

- **Salsa, bottled:** 4 weeks, opened

There's no reason to confuse the keto diet, but it does take some planning. Use these keto tips to boost energy, weight loss, mental focus, and more, and you'll be on your way.

9 ESSENTIAL KETO TIPS FOR BEGINNERS

#1: WATCH OUT FOR HIDDEN CARBS
Even a small amount of carbs can spike your blood sugar, raise your insulin levels, and kick you out of ketosis.

#2: STAY HYDRATED & REPLACE IMPORTANT ELECTROLYTES
Electrolyte and water loss can lead to headaches and muscle aches — two symptoms of the keto flu.

To avoid this, drink plenty of water during your keto transition and replace lost electrolytes with a targeted mineral supplement or by adding sea salt to your water.

#3: CONSIDER INTERMITTENT FASTING
Many people use fasting or intermittent fasting (IF) to get into ketosis faster. Calorie restriction will help you burn through your glycogen stores more quickly, which may mean a quicker transition and fewer keto flu symptoms.

#4: INCLUDE MORE MOVEMENT INTO YOUR DAY
Instead of laying low, try exercising through the discomfort. Light exercise can actually aid in the transition into ketosis by helping you burn through glycogen stores quickly.

#5: STEER CLEAR OF EATING "DIRTY" KETO
Dirty keto foods are often made with processed meats and cheeses and very few nutrient-dense foods. While they're technically within keto guidelines, they're terrible for you and you should only enjoy them in small amounts, if at all.

#6: KEEP YOUR STRESS LEVELS LOW
Yoga, journaling, and meditation are some simple, low-effort ways to lower your stress for the long-term.

#7: GET ENOUGH QUALITY SLEEP
Poor sleep quality or inadequate sleep can throw your hormones out of whack and make it harder for you to lose weight and crush cravings.

#8: TRY EXOGENOUS KETONES
Exogenous ketones are supplemental ketones that help your body transition into ketosis by raising your ketone levels — even if your glycogen stores aren't empty yet.

#9: EAT MORE FAT
If your cravings are getting the best of you during your keto transition, try adding more healthy fats to your day.

Fatty acids from MCT oil (medium chain triglycerides), coconut oil, macadamia nuts, and avocados will help quell cravings and balance your blood sugar levels.

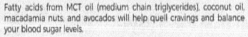

1: Watch Out For Hidden Carbs

2: Stay Hydrated and Replace Important Electrolytes

3: Consider Intermittent Fasting

4: Include More Movement into Your Day

5: Steer Clear of Eating "Dirty" Keto

6: Keep Your Stress Levels Low

7: Get Enough Quality Sleep

8: Try Exogenous Ketones

6.5. Eating away from home

It might sound like a difficult challenge to eat out when keeping to a low-carb, high-fat diet, but it's completely doable with a little bit of preparation.

If you're sharing a quick drink with your working friends, attending family dinner or celebrating your friends' weekend brunch, here's how to handle casual dining while maintaining your ketone levels under control:

- Happy Hour

- Brunch

- Work Lunches

6.6. Fear of eating too much fat

We have repeatedly been advised that fat is unhealthy for several years, and most individuals still believe it. Therefore, many individuals stop consuming fat to be "healthy."

We still encourage them to explain what this entails when dealing with clients who suggest they eat "healthy." The standard replies I hear are the following:

- "I never eat fatty red meat once or twice a week, just chicken or fish."

- "I don't use butter or eggs because my cholesterol is being monitored."

- "My doctor suggested me to use margarine to prevent my family from experiencing heart disease."

- "I'm trying to lose weight, so I calculate fat grams and buy fat-free everything."

Young people usually suffer from signs of stress, weakness, nausea, mood fluctuations, hypoglycemia, insulin intolerance, persistent and insatiable appetite, issues with the gall bladder (gas, bloating, 'acid-reflux,' loose stools), hormonal imbalances, and also loss of menstruation. Women on low-fat diets complain that their hair is dry and brittle and readily falls out, and their skin is dry and wrinkly. And, they almost all try to lose weight, as ridiculous as it sounds!

6.7. Not Eating The Right Fats

A balanced diet and exercise go hand in hand when leading a healthy lifestyle, so keep reading and check out the number one audio fitness app, Aaptiv.

An Important Precursor

Muhlstein mentions the significant differences between good and bad fats to preface this detail and how each one makes us feel. The shortage of safe omega-3 fatty acids from nutrient-dense sources such as flax, chia, fish, almonds, and avocado, and not low fats from packaged and fried foods is likely to result in people having signs and symptoms of fat deficiency in their diet. Healing-all. Double verify that the fats you eat are mostly positive for you.

1. Increase in Appetite

2. Mood Shift

3. Inflammation

4. Dry Skin or Rashes

5. Lowered Immunity

6.8. Not Drinking Enough Water

Here are seven indicators that suggest you may need to start drinking more water to benefit from improved health.

1. Persistent Bad Breath

2. Fatigue

3. Frequent Illness

4. Constipation

5. Poor Skin Health

6. Sugar Cravings

7. Decreased Urination

6.9. Not consuming enough sodium

Here are six little-known risks of limiting too much sodium.

1. Can rise in resistance to insulin

2. No definite advantage of heart attack

3. Increased threat of death due to heart failure

4. LDL (bad) cholesterol and triglycerides can increase.

5. Increased chance of mortality for diabetic persons

6. Lower Hypernatremia Risk (low blood levels of sodium).

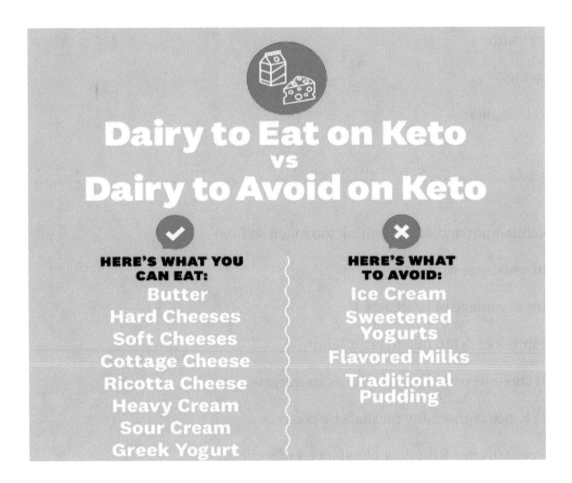

6.11. Snacks

To help you stay on track with your snacking, we put together two comprehensive lists of healthy keto options with goal-oriented subcategories that'll help you find the perfect snack:

The Ready-to-Eat Healthy
Keto Snack List

6.12. Cheat Meals vs. Acceptable Cheats

With your emotional commitment to food, being on a weight loss diet will play havoc because it is normal to have a heavy desire to cheat now and again, even though it could knock you out of ketosis. Carbohydrate limits and, in particular, ketogenic budget diets cause you to change your lifestyle dramatically. For those accustomed to eating candy or many packaged foods, this transition can be daunting and demanding.

How is cheating on a diet?

To get the results you desire, most weight-loss diets come with strict laws or nutritional recommendations that you need to adhere to. To help you shed body fat, these rules and instructions are designed; one is the keto food pyramid. Cheating is every time you attempt to breach all of these laws or instructions and eat anything on the menu that you are pursuing that is not approved. This is why the book related to your low-carb diet of choice is wise to learn because you grasp the values involved.

If you can be kicked out of ketosis by cheating, so why do it?

There are positive and negative motives to cheat on keto, in addition to bumping up leptin production. An impulsive response to temptation is the riskiest reason you find it challenging to give up a candy reward. Cheating at random will ruin your ketogenic diet. Being versatile with keto will help you keep on track and provide you with the practice for the special occasions when you want to eat a few extra maintenance carbohydrates. There are occasional, intentional meals for cheats. They are not a product of poor preparation. Although life will throw you a curveball once in a while that you need to adjust to, these are meals that you thoroughly anticipate what

will happen as a result. You want to take full responsibility for the repercussions.

When the levels of leptin sink too short, deliberate cheating is what you introduce. It would be more frequent and routine with this type of keto cheating than an odd meal higher in carbs. As you get nearer to ideal weight, the satiety you encountered at the beginning of your low-carb diet will begin to fade. You'll need to find a way to raise the leptin as and if it does, and one of the approaches is by implementing strategic hacking. Too much weight for the body.

6.13. Not sleeping enough

Lack of sleep will increase the risk of metabolic complications by throwing off the circadian rhythm. All of your organs observe specific pacing (known as your internal body clock) and upsetting it will place you at a significant disadvantage. With enough sleep, optimum fat loss can only be reached. Sleep, particularly starvation hormones, is also essential for balancing hormones. Sleep influences both leptin and ghrelin (the hormone that makes you feel hungry) (the hormone that makes you feel full). Your ghrelin goes up, and your leptin levels go down because you're not having enough sleep, which is poor weight loss news.

6.14. Worrying

When addressing weight loss challenges, depression is a vital aspect. Your body releases a chemical called cortisol when you're mentally or physically stressed out.

The Cortisol Role

The warning hormone known as the tension hormone is cortisol. When you're under pressure or in a fight-or-flight condition, it's one of the top hormones that the body produces. During the body's response to stress, cortisol can pump glucose into the muscles. It plays a significant role in keeping you alert, awake, encouraged, and it's vital for survival. It is also responsible for accumulating fat in the region of your neck, making it a struggle to lose weight. It is closely related to the development of insulin, too.

When cortisol development becomes chronic due to constant discomfort, the real problem kicks in, then the fat around your stomach begins to rise. Insulin resistance, a metabolic disease that could cause chronic medical problems such as type 2 diabetes, could potentially lead to too much cortisol pulsing into the bloodstream daily.

6.15. Consuming Too Much Protein

Many of the individuals we talk to lament for not being able to

reach ketosis make the mistake of not considering the amount of protein they eat. Their protein intake is much too high, and for some factors that we're going to expand on further, that isn't good.

THE KETOGENIC FOOD PYRAMID

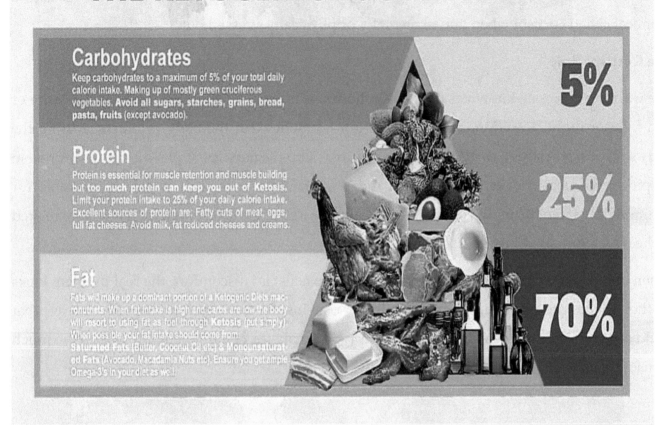

Carbohydrates

Keep carbohydrates to a maximum of 5% of your total daily calorie intake. Making up of mostly green cruciferous vegetables. **Avoid all sugars, starches, grains, bread, pasta, fruits (except avocado).**

5%

Protein

Protein is essential for muscle retention and muscle building but too much protein can keep you out of Ketosis. Limit your protein intake to 25% of your daily calorie intake. Excellent sources of protein are: Fatty cuts of meat, eggs, full fat cheeses. Avoid milk, fat reduced chesses and creams.

25%

Fat

Fats will make up a dominant portion of a Ketogenic Diets macronutrients. When fat intake is high and carbs are low the body will resort to using fat as fuel through **Ketosis** (put simply) When possible your fat intake should come from: **Saturated Fats** (Butter, Coconut Oil etc) & **Monounsaturated Fats** (Avocado, Macadamia Nuts etc). Ensure you get ample Omega-3's in your diet as well.

70%

We know that 75 percent of the keto diet can come from healthier fats that are not refined, but too many people do not factor protein into the calculation. We've also seen people chowing down on lean chicken breast and broccoli while attempting to shed weight and add muscle. Uh, don't do that!

The crucial point is that fat can be the primary macronutrient on a ketogenic diet, unlike many typical low carb diets on which protein dominates.

Specifically, about 20 percent of the macros should be protein. Only enough to conserve lean mass and resist the degeneration of cells. Not so much that it becomes the primary source of food for the body by a mechanism called gluconeogenesis.

6.16. Consuming Too Many Carbs

It would help if you had the perfect mix of carbs, fats and proteins to get through ketosis. That leads to a common question: how much carbohydrates do you consume with keto?

You can consume about 100-150 carbs a day in a Typical American Diet (SAD) and still be considered low-carb. Sadly, this would not turn the body into a fat-burning state of ketosis. Your carb count would be much smaller on the keto diet, often about 25-50 grams of carbs a day.

6.17. Not Getting Enough Exercise

Chronic cardio is the most significant kind of workout exploited by those seeking to lose weight. Your appetite is boosted by repetitive exercise activity, so your body feels depleted and needs the calories back. And your genetics will always prevail in the war between your willpower and your biology. To compensate for the extra calories lost, you'll end up overeating.

While any successful exercise generates some level of acute inflammation, prolonged exercise may cause systemic, internal inflammation and oxidative stress.

6.18. Not Planning Your Meals

As the safest dietary solution, a rising portion of the natural health community endorses the ketogenic diet meal plan. Navigating how to set up foods to support ketosis is the most significant problem people have.

You'll take your particular metabolism into account when preparing meals on a ketogenic diet meal schedule. Some individuals do well with extended fasting, where they go without a calorie supply for 16-18 hours. To retain healthy blood sugar and boost ketones correctly, other people who have adrenal exhaustion can need to eat every 4 hours or so. Not scheduling your meal schedule is the greatest mistake you make.

6.19. Benefits Of Planning Meals

Meal preparation is a critical component of a balanced diet, and batch cooking has many advantages. Even if you're a veteran of

healthy eating, I would strongly advise you to take half an hour a week to prepare your family's healthy meals that week.

The advantages of meal preparation are numerous, including:

1. Save Money

2. Eat Real Food

3. Don't Waste Food

4. Less Stress

5. Save Time

6. Add Variety

6.20. Meal Plan Ideas To Make It Easy

It may sound daunting to turn over to a ketogenic diet, but it does not have to be challenging.

This is why the safest way to lose weight on a ketogenic diet effectively is to adhere to keto-friendly diets and eliminate products high in carbohydrates.

SIMPLE KETO MEAL PLAN #1

BREAKFAST:
- Coffee (Plain, with Heavy cream, or Half & Half)
- 2 Eggs fried in 1-2 tbsp butter/coconut oil/ bacon fat
- 1/2 Avocado
- 2 Slices of Bacon

LUNCH:
Cobb Salad with Ham, Eggs, Bacon, Cheese, and Grilled Chicken (or another source of Protein). Use Ranch as dressing to keep the carbs low.

DINNER:
Egg Roll in a Bowl with optional keto / low carb condiments, such as Sesame seeds, dried seaweed, furikake, sriracha, and egg (recipe on my site: www.ketofy.me)

SNACK: Pork Rinds with Guacamole

@ketofy.me

SIMPLE KETO MEAL PLAN #3

BREAKFAST:
- Cream Cheese Pancakes with SF Syrup
- 2 Slices of Bacon
- Black Coffee or Unsweetened Tea (half and half / heavy cream is optional)

LUNCH:
- Grilled, Baked or Pan fried Salmon (or protein of choice) with Roasted Brussel Sprouts with Butter. You can also try Asparagus, Broccoli or Zucchini.

DINNER:
Chicken Caesar Salad with Romaine Lettuce, Bacon, and Grated Parmesean. Instead of croutons, use baked cheese crisps! Find dressing under 2g carbs per tbsp.

SNACK: Walnuts with SF Chocolate or Dark Chocolate (check nutrition info!)

Meal Plan by @ketofy.me

EASY KETO MEAL PLAN

BREAKFAST:
- **Cream Cheese Pancakes** with Sugar Free Syrup (such as @ChocZero)

LUNCH:
- **Lettuce Wrapped Sub Sandwich** with your choice of protein, low carb vegetables, and keto condiments.

DINNER:
- **Taco Salad** with your marinated (keto style) protein of choice, lettuce, cheese, pico de gallo, sour cream, and guacamole. For crunch, you can toast some @cutdacarb or add cheese crisps on top of your salad.

SNACK:
- Blackberries, Raspberries, or Strawberries with Homemade Whipped Cream

KETO MEAL PLAN WITH MACROS

BREAKFAST
- EGG OMELETTE
  - 3 eggs, scrambled
  - 2oz Ham
  - 1-2oz Mozarella Cheese
  - 50g Mushrooms
  - 1 cup Spinach
  - 1 tbsp butter (or oil for frying)

  MACROS:
  4 NC / 39P / 33F / 450 CALS

LUNCH
- PROTEIN STYLE BURGER
  - 100g Ground Beef (85/15)
  - 3-4 Lettuce Leaves (to wrap)
  - 1 Full Fat Cheese Slice
  - 15g Tomato
  - 10g Onions
  - 1 tbsp Full Fat Mayo
  - Pickles / Mustard / SF Ketchup

  MACROS:
  6 NC / 33P / 23F / 400 CALS

DINNER
- CREAMY GARLIC MUSHROOM CHICKEN
  - Recipe on my site: WWW.KETOFY.ME

  MACROS (PER SERVING):
  3 NC / 45P / 23F / 400 CALS

ALL VALUES ARE APPROXIMATE. CREATED BY LELE @KETOFY.M

6.21. Common Mistakes Made By Beginners

To better ensure that you are following this strategy as safely as possible, avoid the following common keto pitfalls:

1. Very fast too rapidly, cutting your carbohydrates and growing your fat

2. Not Enough Water Drinking on Keto

3. Not getting dressed for the Keto Flu

4. Forgetting to eat Omega-3 Fatty Acids-rich foods

5. Enough not to salt your meal

6. Doing it alone for the Doc and not clearing the diet

7. Your Veggie Consumption is not paying heed

8. Getting caught up in Carb-Counting and denying that it cares for food safety.

6.22. Measurements Conversion Tables

COOKING CONVERSION CHART

Measurement

CUP	ONCES	MILLILITERS	TABLESPOONS
8 cup	64 oz	1895 ml	128
6 cup	48 oz	1420 ml	96
5 cup	40 oz	1180 ml	80
4 cup	32 oz	960 ml	64
2 cup	16 oz	480 ml	32
1 cup	8 oz	240 ml	16
3/4 cup	6 oz	177 ml	12
2/3 cup	5 oz	158 ml	11
1/2 cup	4 oz	118 ml	8
3/8 cup	3 oz	90 ml	6
1/3 cup	2.5 oz	79 ml	5.5
1/4 cup	2 oz	59 ml	4
1/8 cup	1 oz	30 ml	3
1/16 cup	1/2 oz	15 ml	1

Temperature

FAHRENHEIT	CELSIUS
100 °F	37 °C
150 °F	65 °C
200 °F	93 °C
250 °F	121 °C
300 °F	150 °C
325 °F	160 °C
350 °F	180 °C
375 °F	190 °C
400 °F	200 °C
425 °F	220 °C
450 °F	230 °C
500 °F	260 °C
525 °F	274 °C
550 °F	288 °C

Weight

IMPERIAL	METRIC
1/2 oz	15 g
1 oz	29 g
2 oz	57 g
3 oz	85 g
4 oz	113 g
5 oz	141 g
6 oz	170 g
8 oz	227 g
10 oz	283 g
12 oz	340 g
13 oz	369 g
14 oz	397 g
15 oz	425 g
1 lb	453 g

Chapter 7: Top 10 Keto Recipes

7.1. Keto Tacos

(Ready in 1 Hour, Serves: 8, Difficulty: Normal)

Ingredients

Cheese Taco Shells

- 2 cups Cheddar cheese , shredded

Taco Meat

- 1 pound Ground beef

- 2 tablespoon Homemade Taco Seasoning

- 1/4 cup Water

- Toppings for taco: Sour cream, avocado, cheese, lettuce, etc. optional

Instructions

1. Preheat the oven to 350F.

2. Place a 1/4 cup pile of cheese 2 inches apart on a baking sheet lined with parchment paper or a silicone pad. Lightly press the cheese down so that it produces one layer.

3. Place the baking sheet in the oven and bake until the cheese's edges are brown, or for 5-7 minutes.

4. For 1-2 minutes, let the cheese cool until it is solid enough to raise but still bendable. Raise the cheese and put it on two cups above the handle of a spoon or other balanced utensils.

5. Let the cheese cool, and then cut it.

6. As the cheese taco shells begin to be fried, put the ground beef in a skillet over medium-high heat until it is fully cooked through.

7. Drain the beef from the oil and then apply the homemade seasoning to the taco. Pour water into the pan and mix all in it.

8. Simmer for 5 minutes or until the liquid is thoroughly heated.

9. Top with your taco toppings by adding meat to the taco shells.

7.2. Loaded Cauliflower (Low Carb, Keto)

(Ready in 20 Mins, Serves: 4, Difficulty: Normal)

Ingredients

- 1 pound cauliflower

- 4 ounces sour cream

- 1 cup grated cheddar cheese

- 2 slices bacon cooked and crumbled

- 2 tablespoons chives snipped

- 3 tablespoons butter

- 1/4 teaspoon garlic powder

- salt and pepper to taste

Instructions

1. Cut the cauliflower into florets and add them to a healthy bowl in the microwave. Apply two teaspoons of water and cover with cling film. Microwave for 5-8 minutes before fully cooked and tender, depending on your microwave. Drain the excess water and allow for a minute or two to remain uncovered. (Alternatively, steam the traditional way with the cauliflower. After boiling, you can need to drain a little water from the cauliflower.)

2. In a food processor, add the cauliflower and cook until soft. Add the sugar, garlic powder, sour cream, and blend until the mashed potatoes' consistency is close. Remove the mashed cauliflower and apply most of the chives to a dish, leaving some to be added later to the end. Apply half the cheddar cheese and blend it up by hand. With salt and pepper, season.

3. Place the remaining cheese, remaining chives and bacon on top of the loaded cauliflower. To melt the cheese, bring it back in the microwave or place the cauliflower under the broiler for a few minutes.

4. Serves four persons at 4.6g of net carbs.

7.3. Low Carb Pecan Pie (Using Gelatin)

(Ready in 1 Hour, Serves: 10, Difficulty: Normal)

Equipment

- 8-inch pie pan

Ingredients

Crust

- 1 Keto Pie Crust

Filling

- 3/4 cup unsalted butter

- 1/2 cup erythritol

- 1 3/4 cup heavy whipping cream

- 1/2 tsp pink salt

- 15 drops liquid stevia

- 1 1/2 tsp beef gelatin powder

- 1 large egg, room temperature

- 1 1/2 cups raw pecans, roughly chopped

Instructions

1. The oven should be preheated to 350 degrees F. Bake the pie

crust and let it cool for 8-10 minutes.

2. In a large saucepan, melt the butter and erythritol over medium-low heat. Cook, frequently stirring, for 6-8 minutes, until golden brown.

3. Add 1 1/2 cups of cream slowly and bring to a simmer for 15-20 minutes, until thickened and caramel color.

4. Remove the pan from the heat and stir in the stevia and vanilla extract. Set to cool aside. Meanwhile, flower gelatin for 5 minutes in the remaining cold cream.

5. In a clean bowl, whisk the egg gently. Slowly stir in 1/4 cup of caramel sauce, continually whisking to temper the egg. Slowly whisk in the remaining caramel sauce, then add the blooming gelatin.

6. Layer the bottom with chopped pecans from the cooled crust. Pour the ingredients in a bowl mixture over top of the pecans and crust, trying to cover all the pecans.

7. Cover the crust edges with plastic wrap or a pie shield, so it doesn't burn. Bake for 45-55 minutes until stuffing is set.

8. Leave to cool for 20 minutes right before serving. Best stored on the counter for up to three days or in the refrigerator up to ten.

7.4. Easy Keto Pumpkin Pie

(Ready in 55 Mins, Serves: 8, Difficulty: Normal)

Equipment

- 9-inch Pie Pan
- Rolling Pin
- Food Processor or Electric Mixer

Ingredients

Crust

- 1 Recipe Keto Pie Crust

Filling

- 2 large eggs

- 1/2 cup erythritol

- 1.5 tablespoons Pumpkin Pie Spice

- 1/2 teaspoon Pink Himalayan Salt

- 1 can 100% pumpkin puree 15 ounce

- 1 teaspoon vanilla extract

- 1/2 cup Heavy Cream

- Liquid Stevia Optional

Instructions

1. Following these instructions, render the sweet Keto Pie Crust.

2. Using a hand mixer or comb, beat all the ingredients together. Eggs, pumpkin pie spice, salt, pumpkin puree, erythritol, vanilla and heavy cream are also used. If required, throw in extra stevia for added sweetness.

3. Lower the oven temperature to 350 degrees until the pie crust is finished baking.

4. To the partially baked pie crust, apply the filling. To stop burns when appropriate, cover the edges with aluminum foil. Bake at 350 for 30-35 minutes until the filling has set and gently jiggles.

5. Enable the pie to cool completely, then switch it to the refrigerator to finish cooling when the pie is cooled, slice and eat.

6. Up to 5 days in the refrigerator or three weeks in the fridge.

7.5. Keto Dark Chocolate Pie

(Ready in 1 Hour, Serves: 8, Difficulty: Normal)

Equipment

- 10 inch tart pan

Ingredients

- 1 Low Carb Sweet Crust

Filling

- 1/4 cup butter

- 1 cup heavy whipping cream

- 4 oz. unsweetened bakers chocolate, chopped

- 2 tbsp. erythritol

- 1/4 tsp liquid stevia

- 1 tsp vanilla extract

- 1/4 tsp pink salt

- 3 large eggs, room temperature

- 1 cup raw pecans, chopped

Instructions

Crust

1. Roll in a 12-inch round with the pastry dough. Move it and force it into the corners and up the pan's sides to a 10-inch tart pan. Trim the pastry's top edge so that it is level with the tart plate. 30 minutes to relax.

2. Preheat the oven to 375° F. On a baking sheet, position the tart pan.

3. Over the tart, lay a sheet of parchment and carefully mold it into the sides of the plate. Combine with pie weights, rice, dried beans, and simmer for 10-15 minutes or until brown on the sides.

4. Remove the parchment and bake an extra 4-5 more minutes. Enable it to cool while the filling is being made.

Filling

1. Sprinkle the sliced pecans on the bottom of the crust with an even layer.

2. In a saucepan set over a medium-low flame, heat the heavy cream and butter until it melts and starts to boil. Remove and add the chocolate from the heat and mix until melted and smooth.

3. When well absorbed, apply the erythritol, vanilla, stevia, and salt and whisk. In a small cup, beat the eggs until mixed and slowly add them to the mixture of chocolate, whisking until fully blended.

4. Through the cooled tart container, pour the filling. Bake until the filling is set and mildly puffy, for 15-25 minutes.

5. Let the tart cool completely and, if needed, dust with cocoa powder or Erythritol powder before serving.

7.6. Creamy Cauliflower Mash and Keto Gravy

(Ready in 1 Hour, Serves: 4, Difficulty: Normal)

Ingredients

Creamy Mash Cauliflower

- 5 cups cauliflower chopped
- 1/4 cup Heavy Whipping Cream
- 3 tbsp. Butter
- 5 cloves garlic minced
- 2 tsp Dried Rosemary
- 3 tbsp. parmesan
- 1/2 tsp pepper
- Pink Himalayan Salt (to taste)

Instructions

1. Chop up 5 of the fresh cauliflower cups.

2. Bring the pot of water to a boil, add the cauliflower and simmer for 15 minutes or until the cauliflower is tender.

3. Drain and put the cauliflower in the processor.

4. Cook the butter, garlic and rosemary over medium heat in a saucepan until fragrant.

5. To make a processor, add melted butter, thyme and herbs and pulse several times until well mixed.

6. In the blender, add the milk, parmesan, salt and pepper and heat until smooth and fluffy.

7. Taste for the amount of salt. Serve it hot and drink it!

7.7. Authentic Keto Cornbread

(Ready in 50 Mins, Serves: 12, Difficulty: Normal)

Equipment

- Electric Hand Mixer
- 9x13 Casserole Dish

Ingredients

- 2 cups Almond Flour
- 1/4 cup Coconut flour
- 3 tsp Baking powder
- 1 tsp Pink Himalayan Salt
- 3 large eggs
- 1/2 cup butter, melted
- 1/4 cup sour cream
- 25 drops Liquid Stevia
- 1 cup Shredded Cheddar Cheese
- 2/3 can baby corn, roughly chopped

Instructions

1. Preheat the oven to 350 and grease a casserole dish of 9 inches.

2. Combine the almond flour, baking powder, coconut flour, and salt in a medium bowl. Together, whisk and set aside.

3. Combine the eggs, melted butter, whipped cream, and liquid stevia in a wide bowl. Whisk until wholly embedded. When you mix, add the dry ingredients in two batches to the wet one.

4. Fold in the cheddar cheese and cut the baby corn into pieces. For 37-40 minutes, switch to a casserole dish and bake.

5. Enable 15 minutes to cool and slice it into 12 pieces.

7.8. Bacon Wrapped Stuffed Jalapeno Poppers

(Ready in 30 Mins, Serves: 18, Difficulty: Normal)

Ingredients

- 9 jalapeno peppers

- 8 oz. cream cheese, softened

- 1/4 cup salsa Verde

- 1/2 cup shredded cheddar cheese

- 9 slices bacon cut in half

Instructions

1. Break the jalapenos in half, and all the seeds are removed.

2. In a shallow bowl, combine the cream cheese, salsa Verde & shredded cheddar. Attach to a pastry bag or a robust 1-quart zip lock bag until combined and cut off one corner so that the cheese can be pushed out of the opening and onto the peppers. Cover the peppers with a combination of cheese.

3. Meanwhile, cook the bacon for a few minutes in the microwave or saute pan before it begins to brown a bit, but it is still smooth and pliable.

4. Cool, and then cover each half of the jalapeno in one bacon slice. Protect yourself with a toothpick. Place on a baking sheet (with sides) lined with foil and bake for 15 minutes in a preheated 375-degree oven.

5. Set the oven to broil and cook for 2-3 minutes, closely watching to ensure that they do not burn! This offers an excellent roasted taste to the peppers and guarantees that your bacon will be crisp.

6. Before eating, take the jalapeno poppers from the oven and cool slowly. Super low carb and tasty!!!!

7.9. Keto Broccoli Salad

(Ready in 1 Hour 12 minutes, Serves: 6, Difficulty: Hard)

Ingredients

- 2 heads fresh broccoli, cut into florets
- 1 cup mayonnaise
- 1 tbsp. apple cider vinegar
- 1 tsp lemon juice
- 1/2 tsp pink Himalayan salt
- 1/2 tsp black pepper
- 8 slices bacon, cooked and crumbled
- 1/2 cup sunflower seeds

Instructions

1. In boiling water, blanch the broccoli for 1 minute. Drain with cool water and shower.

2. Mix the mayonnaise, vinegar & lemon juice in a large bowl. Mix well.

3. Combine the broccoli, bacon, and seeds in a large dish. Drizzle with the amount of sauce desired.

4. Before you eat, refrigerate for at least 1 hour. Until eating, toss again to cover. Store it in the refrigerator for up to 2 days.

(Ready in 35 Minutes, Serves: 3, Difficulty: Hard)

Ingredients

- 3 cups frozen green bean

- 1/2 cup white onion chopped

- 4 cloves garlic minced

- 2 tbsp. Butter

- 1/4 cup Heavy Whipping Cream

- 1/2 cup chicken stock

- 1/2 cup mushrooms

- 1/2 tsp xanthan gum

- 1/2 tsp Pink Himalayan Salt

- 1/2 tsp pepper

- 1 oz. Pork Rinds

Instructions

1. Frozen green beans thaw (you can microwave them for 5 minutes to heat them through). If you use fresh green beans, make sure that the ends are snapped and boiled to cook them.

2. Chop up the white onions, mushrooms and garlic.

3. Attach two teaspoons. In a saucepan, apply butter and cook over low heat.

4. Attach the onion, mushroom and garlic and roast until the mushrooms are cooked fragrant.

5. Add the stock of cream and chicken and bring to a boil.

6. Turn down to boiling until cooked and allow to simmer for 10-15 minutes.

7. Stir in the xanthan gum and stir until the sauce is thick.

8. Apply the cream sauce to the green beans and coat them thoroughly.

9. Transfer to a skillet with green beans and cover with crumbled rinds of pork.

10. Place it in a 350-degree oven for 10 minutes. For two minutes, broil.

11. Serve it hot and enjoy!

Chapter 8: 30 days Keto Meal Plan

In this chapter we will discuss a 30 days meal plan for Keto diet.

WEEK 1

MON	B: Smashed Avocado & Eggs / L: Bacon & Cheddar Soup / D: Spicy Tacos
TUE	B: Keto Coffee & Walnuts / L: Spicy Tacos / D: Chicken Curry on Cauliflower Rice
WED	B: Cheesy Keto Omelette / L: Chicken Curry on Cauliflower Rice / D: Keto Beef Zoodles
THU	B: Keto Coffee & Walnuts / L: Bacon & Cheddar Soup / D: Keto Beef Zoodles
FRI	B: Smashed Avocado & Eggs / L: Spicy Tacos / D: Chicken Caesar Salad

WEEK 2

MON	B Keto Coffee & Almonds / L: Chicken & Avocado Soup / D: Mexican Beef Skillet
TUE	B: Cheesy Keto Omelette / L: Mexican Beef Skillet / D: Garlic Chicken Zoodles
WED	B: Keto Coffee & Almonds / L: Garlic Chicken Zoodles / D: Piccante Tuna Lettuce Wraps
THU	B: Smashed Avocado & Eggs / L: Chicken & Avocado Soup / D: Sweet & Sour Beef
FRI	B: Keto Coffe & Almonds / L: Piccante Tuna Lettuce Wraps / D: Garlic Chicken Zoodles

WEEK 2

MON	B: Raspberry Vanilla Smoothie / L: Piccante Tuna Lettuce Wraps / D: Parmesan Chicken
TUE	B: Smashed Avocado & Eggs / L: Spicy Tacos / D: Chicken Curry on Cauliflower Rice
WED	B: Keto Coffee & Walnuts / L: Bacon & Cheddar Soup / D: Spicy Tacos
THU	B: Raspberry Vanilla Smoothie / L: Piccante Tuna Lettuce Wraps / D: Parmesan Chicken
FRI	B: Hard Boiled Eggs & Avocado / L: Bacon & Cheddar Soup / D: Spicy Tacos

WEEK 4

MON	B: Blueberry Walnut Smoothie / L: Bacon & Cheddar Soup / D: Steak & Sweet Potato
TUE	B: Smashed Avocado & Eggs / L: Steak & Sweet Potato / D: Chicken Caesar Salad
WED	B: Keto Coffee & Walnuts / L: Chicken Caesar Salad / D: Mexican Beef Skillet
THU	B: Blueberry Walnut Smoothie / L: Smoked Salmon Wraps / D: Chicken Caesar Salad
FRI	B: Hard Boiled Eggs & Avocado / L: Blueberry Walnut Smoothie / D: Chicken Caesar Salad

Conclusion:

There are many food choices available to encourage women over 50 to lose weight and sustain healthier lifestyles, but the keto diet has become one of the most common. It can be tough to regulate weight gain by slowing the metabolism combined with less exercise, muscle degeneration, and the potential for enhanced cravings.

Eating a great combination of greens, lean meat, and unprocessed carbs is an essential element to note. Merely adhering to whole foods is the most effective way to consume a balanced diet, mostly because it is a healthy solution. It is important to remember that ketogenic diets are impossible to complete. For this cause, as mentioned in this book, the safest advice is to find a safe way of eating that fits you.

CPSIA information can be obtained
at www.ICGtesting.com
Printed in the USA
BVHW051047150221
600147BV00011B/949